Feminism, Interrupted

'A well-argued, no-nonsense account, and essential reading for anyone interested in the state of feminism today.'

Stella Dadzie, co-author of *The Heart of the Race: Black Women's Lives in Britain*

'*Feminism, Interrupted* is a lucid and passionate call to action by one of our most dynamic young feminists. Olufemi's manifesto is for a truly radical feminism that liberates us all. If you call yourself a feminist, you need to read this book.'

Alison Phipps, author of *Me, Not You: The Trouble with Mainstream Feminism*

'Lola offers a crucial vision that imagines beyond racist, capitalist solutions to oppression ... the necessity of this book cannot be overstated for those who call themselves feminists and those who eschew feminism as it presents itself.'

Suhaiymah Manzoor-Khan, author of *Postcolonial Banter*

Outspoken by Pluto
Series Editor: Neda Tehrani

Platforming underrepresented voices; intervening in important political issues; revealing powerful histories and giving voice to our experiences; Outspoken by Pluto is a book series unlike any other. Unravelling debates on feminism and class, work and borders, unions and climate justice, this series has the answers to the questions you're asking. These are books that dissent.

Also available:

Mask Off
Masculinity Redefined
JJ Bola

Border Nation
A Story of Migration
Leah Cowan

Behind Closed Doors
Sex Education Transformed
Natalie Fiennes

Lost in Work
Escaping Capitalism
Amelia Horgan

Split
Class Divides Uncovered
Ben Tippet

Feminism, Interrupted

Disrupting Power

Lola Olufemi

First published 2020 by Pluto Press
345 Archway Road, London N6 5AA

www.plutobooks.com

British Library Cataloguing in Publication Data
A catalogue record for this book is available from the British Library

ISBN   978 0 7453 4006 7   Paperback
ISBN   978 1 7868 0592 8   PDF eBook
ISBN   978 1 7868 0594 2   Kindle eBook
ISBN   978 1 7868 0593 5   EPUB eBook

This book is printed on paper suitable for recycling and made from
fully managed and sustained forest sources. Logging, pulping and
manufacturing processes are expected to conform to the environmen-
tal standards of the country of origin.

Typeset by Stanford DTP Services, Northampton, England

Simultaneously printed in the United Kingdom and United States of
America

'Imagine otherwise. Remake the world. Some of us have never had any other choice.' – *Christina Sharpe*

'If you are not the free person you want to be you must find a place to tell the truth about that. To tell how things go for you.' – *Anne Carson*

Contents

Acknowledgements

To Amy Clark and Amelia Horgan, my first readers – thank you. Amy, this book would not exist without your eyes, even though you will deny it.

To Neda Tehrani, for dropping into my inbox and guiding me through this process.

To my family, for giving me the space to write.

This book has many voices in it. Thank you to everyone who agreed to speak to me, in person and online, it was an honour to listen to and read your words. There is no way I can do justice to the conversations we had.

In her poem, *the lost women* Lucille Clifton writes 'where are my gangs/my teams/my mislaid sisters?' I know mine and they are what keep me thinking about feminist futures. Thank you for knowingly and unknowingly guiding my thinking, your unwavering support, your many pep talks: Sandy O, Sarah Lasoye, Christine Pungong, Waithera Sebatindira, Abeera Khan, Miriam Gauntlett, Kate Litman, Hareem Ghani, Diamond Abdulrahim, Micha Frazer-Carroll, Jun Pang, Suhaiymah Manzoor-Khan, Siyang Wei, Victoria Braid, Priscilla Mensah, Nydia Swaby, Arenike Adebajo, Christie Costello, Vera Chapiro, Hattie Read, Leo Would, Ellie Byrne, Amelia Oakley, Martha PW, Claire Sosienski-Smith, the many members of FLY, CUSU Womcam and Sisters Uncut.

It was black feminist theory from across the globe that woke me up to the violence and misery of this world and provided the most creative, comprehensive and transformative solutions to it. It gave me the sincerity that is at the core of my politics. It allowed me to *live* in a different way. Every single idea and thought in this book would not have been possible without it. Anybody who is interested in building a just future for all must seriously engage with that canon, in all its forms. It would be unwise not to.

Introduction: Feminist work is justice work

'And what does the gift of feminism consist of if not a certain bundle of ways of thinking historically, ways of seeing, ways of hoping?' – Vikki Bell

Feminism is a political project about what *could be*. It's always looking forward, invested in futures we can't quite grasp yet. It's a way of wishing, hoping, aiming at everything that has been deemed impossible. It's a task that has to be approached seriously. This book is for anyone who is beginning to think critically. Feminist histories are unwieldy; they cannot and should not be neatly presented. I hope this book makes you think about the limits of this world and the possibilities contained in the ones we could craft together. I hope it makes you want to read more and become more familiar with radical feminist thought and practice. If this book makes you pick up another book, or watch a documentary, search the archive, reach for a poetry book – if it sparks or reignites your interest in feminism, then it has served its purpose.

Everybody has a story about how they arrived and keep arriving at radical politics. Some of us are politicised by the trauma of our own experiences, by wars waged in our names, by our parents and lovers, by the internet. It's useful to share the ways we become politicised if only because it helps politicise others. Growing up as a young black woman, I felt the oppressive way the world was organised with my body and through

1

interpersonal relations long before I could articulate what those feelings meant. Revelling in the discovery of the word 'feminism' and its history as a political practice in my early teenage years at school, I found a personal freedom. I read ferociously. Black feminism, Liberal feminism, Marxist feminism, Anarcha-feminism, Eco-feminism. Feminism opened up my world. I saw in it, conflicting theorists and activists, all giving their ideas about the way the world should be. Perhaps most memorably, it released me from the desire to comply with the world as it is. This meant many things for me as an individual; feminism allowed me to be wayward, the wrong kind of woman, deviant. It took me longer to realise that true liberation meant extending this newfound freedom beyond myself. Just because I felt freer in some respects, did not mean I was free.

The material conditions of my life were still determined by the same systems; poverty and racism still trapped the women around me. Disparities in healthcare, education, public services and access to resources limited the possibility for any kind of expansive existence. I saw how black women were locked out of womanhood as defined by a white supremacy and how anyone outside of those accepted boundaries simply did not exist in the eyes of mainstream feminism. I began to understand how my own rebellion, the defiance instilled in me by the feminists I admired, was raced and classed. I read about how freedom requires upheaval and must be fought for, not romanticised. It was during this period that I realised that feminism was not simple. There were no pre-given solutions. The 'answer', if there was one, required us to place different feminisms in conversation and necessitated a radical flexibility in our organising. Feminism was complicated and messy in ways that made me reconsider my foundational political beliefs: equality versus liberation, reform versus abolition. Feminism meant *hard work*, the kind done without reward or recognition, the kind that requires an unshakeable belief in its importance, the kind that is long and tiresome, but that creates a sense of purpose. It proposed a new way of being that transformed the way I looked at the world.

The feminists I admired argued that the abolition of all prevailing systems of violence was crucial to any feminist future. They called for a revolution in the way we think about ourselves and others. Their critiques of the state, capitalism, the family, white supremacy, sex and education encouraged in me a rejection of what was expected. They provided a place to say the unsayable. bell hooks writes about how she came to theory 'desperate, wanting to comprehend – to grasp what was happening around and within me'.[1] The same can be said for many young women who come to theory to be given a blueprint for a better world; who come to theory looking for a way to be changed.

I knew I had to choose what kind of feminism would form the basis of my understanding. My experiences had taught me that nothing should be taken for granted; there was no coherence or consensus on accepted principles in the feminist movement. If anything, it was defined by conflict. The decision to practice a radical feminism was crucial because I became aware of how it separated those wanting to create a new vision for the world from those merely wanting to climb the rungs of power.

Who's the boss?

There is a divide playing out in the mainstream. The emergence of neo-liberal feminism or 'boss girl feminism', driving many contemporary discussions, clashes with a radical and critical vision of feminism. Broadly speaking, neo-liberalism refers to the impo-

---

1   bell hooks, 'Theory as Liberatory Practice,' in *Teaching to Transgress: Education as the Practice of Freedom* (New York: Routledge, 1994), pp. 59–75.

sition of cultural and economic policies and practices by NGOs and governments in the last three to four decades that have resulted in the extraction and redistribution of public resources from the working class upwards, decimated infrastructures of social care through austerity measures, privatised the welfare state and individualised the ways we relate to one another. The neo-liberal model of feminism argues that 'inequality' is a state that can be overcome in corporate environments without over-hauling the system, centralises the individual and their personal choices, misguidedly imagines that the state can grant liberation, seeks above all to protect the free market and fails to question the connection between capitalism, race and gendered oppression. This model of feminist thought is most appealing to those who have a limited knowledge of radical history and the gains fought and won by activists who dared to demand what was once deemed impossible. The consumerist promise of success that neo-liberal feminism offers is hollow, because it is a superficial promise made only to those who can access it.

White feminist neo-liberal politics focuses on the self as vehicle for self-improvement and personal gain at the expense of others. We are instructed by corporate talking heads to 'lean in' into a capitalist society where power equals financial gain. This model works best for wealthy white women, who are able to replace men in a capital structure. Liberal feminism's obsession with getting women 'to the top' masks a desire to ensure that the current system and its violent consequences remain intact. It invisibilises the women of colour, low paid workers and migrant women who must suffer so that others may 'succeed.' It makes their exploitation a natural part of other women's achievements. In this approach there is no challenge to hegemony, only acquiescence. The boardroom has become a figurative battle-ground upon which many stake their feminist aspirations. If

4

we are to challenge this, we must ask 'what about the fate of the low paid women who clean the boardrooms?' and 'what makes their labour so easily expendable?' A feminism that seeks power instead of questioning it does not care about justice. The decision to reject this way of thinking is also a decision to reject easy solutions. We all have to ask ourselves at some point, who will I be and what will I do? What can my politics help me artic-ulate? What violence will it expose?

All of these questions are crucial to every young feminist because by choosing a feminist politics that is critical, you are making a commitment to a world that has not yet been built. A world other people will tell you that you are foolish to believe in. The decision to shun a simplistic, consumerist and neo-liberal feminism will shake your understandings of the principles that underpin feminist thinking. Refusing neo-liberalism will open you up to a world where 'feminist' means much more than 'woman' or 'equality.' Making these connections is crucial to any revolutionary work because it means that nobody is left behind, nobody's exploitation goes unseen. It asks us to practice radical compassion, to refuse to ignore the pain of others. It demands that we see how tackling seemingly unrelated phenomena like prison expansion, the rise of fascism, neocolonialism and climate crisis must also become our priorities.

The task

'Feminist work is justice work.' When I heard this phrase at a university event, something changed. It came to define how I think about feminism and its goals. The phrase stuck with me because it was different to what I saw in the mainstream. 'Feminist work is justice work' proposes that feminism has a purpose beyond just highlighting the ways women are 'discrimi-nated' against. It taught me that feminism's task is to remedy the consequences of gendered oppression through organising and by proposing new ways to think about our potential as human beings. For me, 'justice work' involves reimagining the world we live in and working towards a liberated future for all. But how do we begin to reimagine? We refuse to remain silent about how our lives are limited by heterosexist, racist, capitalist patriarchy. We invest in a political education that seeks above all, to make injustice impossible to ignore. We ensure that nobody is allowed to suffer in silence, that no one's pain goes unseen.

Feminism has re-entered the public imagination in a big way. Where the word was once taboo, young people are being exposed to it now more than ever. We have to ask whether its rebellious roots are still at the core of our understanding. Has feminism lost its radical implications?

Chimamanda Ngozi Adiche's Ted Talk popularised by Beyonce in 2013 was not only a cultural moment, but a good example of how feminism has been packaged and resold to a younger audience. T-shirts and tote bags abound. The feminism on sale was stripped of a structural analysis and instead became solely about behaviours, attitudes and 'teaching' men to be better. This opened the floodgates. Debates about which celebrities identify as 'feminist' took centre stage in magazines, interviews and press junkets. While critiquing this trend is a necessity, it is also important to remember that, when used strategically, public narrative and mainstream discussions can be a useful tool to make oppression visible and give people the strategies to combat it. Cultural conversations about feminism have a purpose; they can do the work of bringing the problem to attention. Artistic creations provide an avenue for reflection on the dynamics that govern our lives. They bolster what Gramsci called 'optimism of the will,' having the courage to believe that a more dignified world is possible, reinvigorating movements that have lost their energy. Pop culture and mainstream narratives can democratise feminist theory, remove it from the realm of the academic and shine a light on important grassroots struggle, reminding us that feminism belongs to no one.

We all begin somewhere. A feminist understanding is not inherent; it is something that must be crafted. Theory does not only mean reading dense academic texts. Theory can be *lived*, held, shared. It is a breathing, changeable thing that can be infused in many political and artistic forms. Learning requires the patience and empathy of those around you and an investment in the importance of radical education. This radical education comes in many forms. When feminism enters the mainstream, it does not automatically lose its meaning or its appeal. What matters is the way it is discussed and whether or not that discussion challenges or affirms the status quo. How often have the articles about feminism in mainstream publications inspired revolt? We have to ask what comes next after identifying the problem. As a starting point, can we move mainstream conversations about period poverty beyond the clutches of feminine hygiene companies and towards the fundamental idea that we cannot tackle this problem without ending austerity? Can we link the public disclosures of trauma facilitated by #MeToo to the fact that many victims and survivors cannot leave violent situations because of the lack of available social housing or domestic violence provisions? Can we use intersectionality as it was intended, a meaningful framework that exposes a matrix of domination, and seeks to improve vital women's services, and not a vehicle for a laundry list of our identities?

Feminist visions

Feminism provokes a kind of feeling, a reaction, repulsion in the eyes of its detractors, and rightfully so. There are men

7

who have built their careers on deriding us, media outlets that gleefully malign the seriousness of the task at hand. In 2018, Sp!ked Magazine ran two articles with the following headlines: 'No, women aren't at risk from men'[2] and 'Not everything is a feminist issue'[3] A great deal of recruitment of young men into fascism and Incel communities relies heavily on disproving or finding the logical 'flaws' in feminist ideology. 'Feminism is cancer' is a common slogan. Feminism is a threat. It is also a call to action. 'How should we think about the world?' remains one of the most important, frustrating, joyful questions to answer because it requires a recognition that our lives, our fate, our successes and disappointments are all connected. When we do feminist work, we are doing the kind of work that changes the world for everybody. It is important to feel free but it is more important to make sure we get free – socially, politically, economically, artistically. Here we see why the decisions we make early on about what kind of feminists we will be are so important; it is vital to correct the misinformation about what it means to be a feminist in theory and in practice.

Imagine this: A world where the quality of your life is not determined by how much money you have. You do not have to sell your labour to survive. Labour is not tied to capitalism, profit or wage. Borders do not exist; we are free to move without consequence. The nuclear family does not exist; children are raised collectively; reproduction takes on new meanings. In this world, the way we carry out dull domestic labour is transformed and nobody is forced to rely on their partner economically to survive. The principles of transformative justice

2   www.spiked-online.com/2018/08/02/no-women-arent-at-risk-from-men/ (last accessed 11/2018).

3   www.spiked-online.com/2018/07/25/not-everything-is-a-feminist-issue/ (last accessed 11/2018).

are used to rectify harm. Critical and comprehensive sex education exists for all from an early age. We are liberated from the gender binary's strangling grip and the demands it places on our bodies. Sex work does not exist because work does not exist. Education and transport are free, from cradle to grave. We are forced to reckon with and rectify histories of imperialism, colonial exploitation, and warfare collectively. We have freedom *to*, not just freedom *from*. Specialist mental health services and community care are integral to our societies. There is no 'state' as we know it; nobody dies in 'suspicious circumstances' at its hands; no person has to navigate sexism, racism, disablism or homophobia to survive. Detention centres do not exist. Prisons do not exist, nor do the police. The military and their weapons are disbanded across nations. Resources are reorganised to adequately address climate catastrophe. No person is without a home or loving community. We love one another, without possession or exploitation or extraction. We all have enough to eat well due to redistribution of wealth and resource. We all have the means and the environment to make art, if we so wish. All cultural gatekeepers are destroyed.

Now imagine this vision not as utopian, but as something well within our reach.

The vision I have presented has its limitations. There are gaps, contradictions and things that have been omitted. But without the capacity to imagine in this way, feminism is purposeless. Let us fight over a vision because our demands must spring from somewhere. This is the task handed down to us and we must approach it with the urgency it demands. We must rise to the challenge with a revolutionary and collective sense of determination; knowing that if we do not see this world, someone else will.

Chapter 1

Know your history

That first person plural voice enabled us to really own the narrative and say, 'This is our history, this is what's happening to us.' Do you remember when we had the launch at the Hammersmith Riverside Studios and that sister stood up in the audience? I think all three of us were there. She was crying and she said 'You know, I've heard these stories around my grandmother's table all my life, but it's the first time I've seen them in writing, and I want to thank you for writing it down.' – Stella Dadzie

Black women's organisations in Britain have therefore created a fundamentally holistic politics of transformation which integrates the individual and the communal, connects the local with the global and meshes the pragmatic with the visionary. It is this philosophical and ideological base which will sustain black women's activism into the next century. – Julia Sudbury

Black women's history travels in whispers and memories recalled around the dining table by mothers and grandmothers and it often dies when those voices leave us. The power of these stories is that they make us feel less alone and give us the courage to act by providing us with a blueprint. This is important for young feminists because there are forces acting on us at all times that tell us that revolution is impossible. These forces take a toll on our bodies, our minds, our sense of ourselves and our understanding of what is possible. History allows us to see that subversion and, more importantly, resistance has always existed. Feminist activists have always pushed boundaries set by the state, by men, by the powerful, and in doing so, laid the foundations for a new world.

Black British feminist organising is not part of our public consciousness and yet it provides one of the most comprehensive examples of nuanced, creative and powerful organising practice. When we think about feminism, we tend not to think of the coalitions built in the United Kingdom by black women who understood the urgency of providing transformative solutions to the problems they faced. Being robbed of this history situates feminism elsewhere; it prevents us from thinking about how to do activism and community work in our own lives. It turns the history of feminism in the UK into a narrative of linear progress led by middle class white women and flattens the complex and interconnected ways that radical, grassroots groups transformed their communities, and in doing so expanded what it meant to be a 'feminist.' When this history is actively erased, not only do we lose out on valuable knowledge, we lose the ability to learn from, expand on and continue the legacy that was forged through struggle. Black British feminist history teaches those of us engaged in feminist organising that we are not the first and we will not be the last, we are simply a continuation of everything that has come before us: our task is to persist.

Part of the reason that much of grassroots organising by black women has been written out of mainstream women's history is the institutionalisation of the study of gender. The academy became the site that defined women's history, but the women most likely to enter academia and carry out this research were not those engaged in movement building at a grassroots level. When the past was reimagined through a specific set of eyes, namely white and middle class, its radical roots disappeared because it became necessary to tell the story of feminist progress. This story was neatly divided into waves characterised by different beliefs and legislative gains. The story goes: First wave feminists fought for the vote and property rights. The second wave broadened the conversation to women's subjugation in the family, the workplace, sexual relations, bodily autonomy and reproductive rights. The third wave was heavily influenced by the advent of the internet, and the emergence of concepts like intersectionality, which became embedded in their feminist ethos. But, it is impossible to create a narrative that does justice to knotty truths lived by feminists of all kinds.

Waves

Separating feminist history into waves often erases the splintered nature of feminist struggles, neglecting the existence of dividing lines across race and class. For example, when white middle class Suffragettes fought for the right to vote in the late nineteenth century and the early twentieth century, they did not consider the women under colonial control subjected to inordinate amounts of violence or the working class women who would not meet the property requirements needed to vote. Many of their arguments were based on the racist assumption that white women deserved the vote before black men.[1] During the 'second wave', black feminists consistently drew attention to the mainstream feminist movement's refusal to examine their complicity in racism and their inability to consider the lives of

---

1   www.nytimes.com/2018/07/28/opinion/sunday/suffrage-movement-racism-black-women.html (last accessed 01/2019).

black women, marked by overlapping and intersecting systems of oppression. Thinking about feminism in waves erases dissenting voices. In the neat retelling of feminist history, black feminism is framed as antagonistic, on the periphery, on the outside trying to get in. Not only is this retelling inaccurate, the 'waves' analogy redefines what counts as feminist work to advancements made solely in relation to rights and legislation, so that slave rebellions orchestrated by black women in European colonies or social and political uprisings against colonial invaders do not constitute 'feminist' history.

During the 70s and 80s, many black British feminist organisers in the UK positioned themselves as belonging to the legacy of resistance work carried out by women from the African continent. They broke waves by redefining who 'counts' as the subject of feminism, ensuring that their feminist practice was about more than just gender. When Stella Dadzie, Suzanne Scafe and Beverly Bryan wrote *Heart of the Race: Black Women's Lives in Britain,* one of the foundational texts charting the formation of the groups central to the Black British feminist movement in Britain, they were not only resisting their own erasure, but challenging narrow conceptions of feminism.

The early 70s saw a number of splinter groups emerge from Black Power and anti-racist movements; there was an appetite for consciousness raising groups that could speak specifically to the concerns of black women and recognise how their concerns differed from those of black men. Black women gathered to organise, provide political education, create resources and support one another. They created spaces of reflection as well as planning, where women's voices were the central contributors to political discussions on the conditions needed for liberation. Olive Morris, a community activist and communist from Brixton was a key figure in the Brixton Black Women's Group (BBWG) established in 1973–4; other members included Gail Lewis, Melba Wilson and Olive Gallimore. BBWG was a socialist group, many of its members prominent in tenants and squatter's campaigns. They helped to establish supplementary schools, black community bookshops, and lobbied for a more critical education that would teach the histories of colonial violence and imperialism that were suppressed by the British government. BBWG campaigned for better childcare provision, reproductive justice, an end to the criminalisation of black people through SUS laws[2] and against virginity testing at Heathrow Airport[3]. Initially, they met at the Sabaar Bookshop on Railton Road until a Black Women's Centre was established in 1979–80. As the work of black women and women of colour continued to grow, the umbrella organisation, The Organisation of Women of African and Asian Descent (OWAAD), was founded in 1978 by fifteen members who met at Warwick University in February 1978. Key figures included Stella Dadzie, Gail Lewis, Olive Morris, Gerlin Bean, Slyvia Eryke, Beverly Bryan and Susanne Scafe among many others.

'We'd come together to discuss how we could mobilise more sisters to take part in the African Students Union, which we all had connections with.'[4] The group united a number of different women's groups with the aim of pooling resources and co-ordinating activism. Many of its members emerged from Marxist, anti-imperialist, anti-racist movements: the work they did in their communities was inseparable from this. They

---

2 Informal name for the law that gave police permission to stop, search and arrest individuals in breach of the Vagrancy Act 1824.

3 In the 1970s, the Home Office subjected a number of South Asian women to invasive virginity tests to prove their eligibility for the visas: www.theguardian.com/uk/2011/may/08/virginity-tests-immigrants-prejudices-britain (last accessed 01/2019).

4 Beverly Bryan, Stella Dadzie and Suzanne Scafe, *Black Women's Lives in Britain* (London: Verso, 2018), p. 165.

used zines, community press and their newsletter, *FOWAAD!*, to communicate their work to the local community. They had an explicitly transnational focus and thought about how to link the liberatory work of African members of the diaspora to work being done on the African continent. There were many kinds of women involved in this organising: mothers, women without children, lesbians and queer women, women who were working class, university educated, and in low paid or precarious work. From this unique position they made visible those rifts and tensions that make it impossible to conceive of feminism as a united or coherent set of practices.

Beyond the self

When black feminists and women of colour organised in the UK, they rejected the idea that feminism was merely about the self, the body or personal liberation. They were working towards collective improvement in material conditions. As well as understanding the need to know themselves as individuals, they identified the social, political and economic structures that oppressed them and targeted this in their campaigning. For example, the two-year Grunwick Strike of 1976, led by South Asian women from India and Pakistan, demanded that working class women be properly compensated for their labour. Groups of low paid women workers went on strike to protest their exploitation at the hands of Grunwick Film Processing Laboratories, who recruited poor South Asian women from former British colonies, assuming they were docile and lacked understanding of labour rights. They were subjected to racism, poor working conditions and unequal pay.[5] When the Trade Union

---

5   www.striking-women.org/module/striking-out/grunwick-dispute (last accessed 01/2019).

Congress, a body set up to protect the rights of workers, withdrew their support for the strike, women led by Jayaben Desai went on hunger strike in protest outside their headquarters in 1977. There is a long history of black women and women of colour mounting organised and strategic campaigning and lobbying efforts in direct response to the dehumanising conditions they were subjected to in and outside of the workplace.

The women central to this kind of campaigning wanted freedom from police harassment and brutality, good working conditions; a just society to raise their families in. Their goals were steeped in the desire to remake the world through their everyday lives. 'We helped to set up and maintain the first Black Bookshop in Brixton, and joined the Railton 4 Campaign over police harassment. We also mobilised the community in Brixton against the practice of setting up disruptive units and the campaign for parental rights.'[6] All of these demands are feminist demands. What their work teaches us is that if feminism is to be useful, it has to mean a change in material circumstance, not only in our local communities, but across the world. For OWAAD, feminist and anti-racist work meant revolution and developing a framework that aligned their organising with those of the so-called 'Third World'. Their work was inspired by revolutionaries engaged in struggles for freedom on the African continent:

> We were influenced far more, at the time, by what was happening in the liberation movements in the African continent. There were more examples of Black women who were active in revolutionary struggles in places like Angola, Mozambique, Eritrea, Zimbabwe and Guinea-Bissau . . . what Somara

---

6 Bryan, Dadzie & Scafe, *The Heart of the Race*, p. 150.

Machel had to say about women's emancipation made a lot more sense to us than what Germaine Greer and other middle class white feminists were saying.[7]

Acts of solidarity and building meaningful links across continents was central to OWAAD'S organisational practice. Through their involvement in the African Students Union, founding members of OWAAD worked alongside groups set up by women from Ethiopia and Eritrea. Forming study groups to read political theory, they worked with groups such as SWAPO and the Zanu Women's League, who put them in contact with women involved in revolutionary struggles on the African continent and set up routes through which to share tactics and resources, and to hold a number of joint activities. Olive Morris travelled to China on a student delegation to the Society for Anglo-Chinese Understanding to discuss socialism, and similarly travelled to Algeria, France, Spain and Hong Kong. This global outlook enabled people to spot the similarities between their struggles and to think about how all lives are structured by the same systems of power. While it is important to start locally and build movements in our communities, the most radical work is work that looks beyond borders and nations, and finds subversive ways to link the work of oppressed people across the world – something we will look at more in the final chapter.

Groups like the BBWG and OWAAD belong to a legacy of black feminist organisers who practiced intersectionality long before it was coined by legal scholar Kimberlé Crenshaw in 1989. They built on the work of communist feminist pioneers like Claudia Jones who urged the Marxist left to recognise the relationship between race, gender and exploitation and argued that: 'the

---

7   Bryan, Dadzie & Scafe, *The Heart of the Race*, p.148–9.

triply oppressed status of negro women is a barometer of the status of all women.'[8] Their activism recognised Audre Lorde's idea that 'there is no such thing as a single issue struggle because we do not live single issue lives,'[9] and embodied the spirit of the Combahee River Collective, a black lesbian feminist collective from Boston. In their seminal statement published in 1977, they argued that: 'No one before has ever examined the multilayered texture of Black Women's lives.'[10]

As black women standing outside the bounds of 'woman-hood' as it was constructed by whiteness, their intention was not simply to be included in the category, but to transform its meaning and potential by remaining attentive to the needs of the communities to which they belonged. The term 'feminist' is often retroactively applied to the work carried out by some of the groups under the OWAAD's umbrella but in *Heart of the Race*, the authors discuss some of the women's difficulties with embracing the term: 'We would not have called ourselves feminists by any means – we didn't go that far for many years. It took us a long time before we worked out a Black women's perspective, which took account of race, class, sex and sexuality.'[11]

For some of the women involved in OWAAD, developing a feminist consciousness was a continuous process. For others, it was what drove them to the work in the first place. Perhaps this

8   Claudia Jones, 'We Seek Full Equality for Women.' in *Claudia Jones: Beyond Containment*, edited by Carole Boyce Davies (Oxfordshire: Ayebia Clarke Publishing Limited, 2010), pp. 86–9.

9   Audre Lorde, 'Learning from the 60s,' in *Sister Outsider: Essays & Speeches by Audre Lorde* (Berkeley, CA: Crossing Press, 2007), p. 138.

10   Combahee River Collective, *The Combahee River Collective Statement: Black Feminist Organizing in the Seventies and Eighties* (Albany, NY: Kitchen Table: Women of Colour Press, 1986).

11   Bryan, Dadzie & Scafe, *The Heart of the Race: Black Women's Lives in Britain*, p. 150

is a useful way to think about what being a feminist means. If we view feminism as an approach, a way to think about the world, it shifts the focus away from words, towards action. Feminist principles are not something that can be 'achieved'. They are cultivated through a reflective process that has no end. They grow, change and take shape as we do.

Movement lessons

In a coffee shop, Gail Lewis, a founding member of BBWG and OWAAD tells me, 'Movements struggle to articulate where they are going as they happen.' Every attempt to retell the history of a movement is a failure because it can never capture everything. But these words open up a space to think about the divisions that marked the Black British feminist movement. As an umbrella organisation, OWAAD's broad focus increased their workload and brought ideological and racial differences to the forefront. Some members were keen to focus on consciousness raising and local issues, while others had a more global outlook; this created tensions around the group's priorities, tactics and focus. The use of political blackness as an organising principle called into question the effectiveness of rhetorics of unity and solidarity. Put simply, it became impossible to do everything and the unpaid labour necessary to keep movements like this alive was incompatible with the demands of wage labour.

OWAAD became unsustainable because the burden of organising fell to a select few, internal hierarchies began to emerge and simply, 'life got in the way'. Many of the women engaged in core organising work stepped back to have children, to get married, travel and pursue careers. At the same time, under the Greater London Council leadership of Ken Livingstone, from 1981–6, grassroots organisations were subsumed into the state structure. New diversity positions in local councils were created alongside a spate of institutional titles that activists were encouraged to pursue, widening the gap between them and the communities they were fighting for.

The issues of queer women, although urgent and politically relevant, were sidelined because activists lacked the language and conviction to understand queerness' relation to feminist work and questions of state violence. Lewis reflects on this: 'We didn't know how to pose it as a political question . . . what do you do with queer life?' Generations later, there has been an attempt to excavate the centrality of lesbian life to organising history and to reflect on the mechanisms that silenced individuals from living queer lives openly and without shame. OWAAD's burdens were many. As a women's group, they were required to prove their political relevancy to men who accused them of division; this resulted in a deep anxiety about the presentation of their work and practices, leading to a culture of silence around questions of sexuality, mandating a negation of queer life.

When we organise as feminists, we have to ask: what are we demanding from ourselves and from others? How is the work being distributed? Gail reflects specifically on what this means for black women organisers: 'Identify how wedded you are to this fantasy and this really oppressive stereotypical myth of the strong black women . . . we lived a version of that and in the end, there were other demands that said no.' Activist work is tireless, but it is important that we do it anyway because it is one of the few methods that provide us with a chance of transforming the way we live.

This is why knowing our history matters, it reminds us of the myriad ways that we can begin to instrumentalise feminist thought and practice to make changes where we are. It helps us improve our own strategies and succeed where other movements did not. It is our job as feminists to rediscover the histories that have been purposefully withheld from us because it is the voices that speak to us from the past that help shape our vision for the future.

Chapter 2

The sexist state

look i get radicalized by love . . .
I get radicalized by love
and by austerity
and by work...
It's easy to get radicalized just by paying attention to
experience – Marion Bell

In 2015, Sister's Uncut, a feminist direct action group, turned the fountains of Trafalgar Square red. 'They cut, we bleed,' they chanted. They marked the closure of over 30 women's refuges since 2010 as a direct result of austerity measures.

The state organises our lives. It defines the parameters of the way we live, from what is legal and illegal, to the medical, social and political services we can access. The state refers to a central organisation that is in charge of everything from welfare and law, to housing and policing. The state is everywhere; its main mouthpiece is the government, which sets the laws we must live by. Academic Wendy Brown argues, 'Despite the almost unavoidable tendency to speak of the state as an "it," the domain we call the state is not a thing, system, or subject but a significantly unbounded terrain of powers and techniques.'[1] Radical

1 Wendy Brown, *States of Injury: Power and Freedom in Late Modernity* (New Jersey: Princeton University Press), p. 174.

feminists have long critiqued the role of the state in propping up and maintaining sexist oppression, exposing how it helps to extend control over our lives and bodies, a control that is relentlessly justified as necessary. Because we imagine state power as inevitable, it seems ludicrous to think about another way we might organise all of the resources listed above. What might a world without a police force look like? How would we organise provisions for housing and welfare without a centralised body?

When feminists call the state 'sexist', they mean that state provision, the allocation of resources and the way oversight is carried out reinforces gendered oppression by restricting women's freedom and ensuring that poor women have no means to live full and dignified lives. Historically, the ways that the state has suppressed women's freedom seem quite clear. From restrictions on voting rights, abortion, rights under marriage and property ownership, we can name the ways the state mobilised its power to ensure women remained so called 'second-class citizens'. Liberal feminism tells us that this was a long time ago and that times have changed. Things are generally better for women than they were 50 years ago. Because we are living in an age where 'gender equality' is a hot topic and public figures and politicians proudly state their feminist credentials, it is now harder to trace the legacy of this repression and to examine the ways that it continues to this day. The state has orchestrated a smokescreen. But what happens when we blow it away?

The equality illusion

Critical feminism argues that state sexism has not lessened, but merely shifted underground and taken a different shape. Perhaps the greatest trick of recent history has been to convince women that the state cares for their well-being and that the state apparatus values gender equity. Articles about gender pay gaps, our first 'feminist' prime minister, Theresa May, and an obsession with the number of female MPs in parliament hide the very insidious ways that the state continues to enable male dominance. For example, in February 2018, the Conservative government introduced their plans to pass a Domestic Violence Bill with the intention of increasing the number of convictions for perpetrators of abuse. Some might view this 'tough' approach to domestic violence as stemming from a care for survivors and a desire to protect them, but it is simply another example of the way the state plays on our anxieties about women's oppression to disguise the enactment of policies that trap women in subordinate positions.

The Domestic Violence Bill is by no means a feminist piece of legislation. Its focus on conviction means an increased police presence, heightening the risk that women who are victims and survivors end up in prison. The bill suggests that in some cases, the deportation of vulnerable survivors to contexts they are wholly unfamiliar with may be the best way of helping them. Research from the Prison Reform Trust has found an increase in the number of survivors being arrested, despite the fact that their partners were the primary aggressors. 57 per cent of women in prison are survivors of domestic abuse.[2] The most pressing issues for survivors is not that their abusers go to prison, but that there is a safety net for them to fall back on that enables them to leave abusive situations. They need refuges, routes to economic stability and adequate welfare support. Yet, in the past ten years, they have been faced with cuts to local authority councils, closures of domestic violence shelters and restrictions on benefits. The

2   www.prisonreformtrust.org.uk/PressPolicy/News/vw/1/ItemID/494 (last accessed 02/2019).

focus on conviction instead of welfare support enables men to continue to exercise power over everything from women's bodies to their finances. This is just one of several examples: when the feminist façade slips, it reveals the women that are harmed and die as a result of state negligence and underfunding. In custody, on the breadline, in the queue for the job centre or the shelter, they know the state's indifference all too well.

Austerity

When successive governments implement violent austerity policies in order to 'balance the budget', it is women who are hit the hardest, because their lives have always been intimately linked to the state. Because women on average earn less than men, they disproportionately depend on the state for a range of services such as child maintenance, legal aid and housing provision. 90 per cent of lone parents are working mothers who, while historically characterised as leeching off the state, are often in low-paid work attempting to provide for their families.[3] Our feminism must centre the material needs of these women and form strategies to secure the redistribution of resources. Building economic justice into feminism is about recognising the deep inequalities that govern the way we live. We have to care about the fate of women in low-paid work, homeless women, women engaged in survival sex work and every other woman the state leaves behind. If we view the state as another arm of patriarchy, as an institution designed to oppress, then we can more clearly see how it mimics the language of freedom and equality while enacting policies that ensure the exact opposite. Although utopian thinking carries us further than the limits of

---

3   www.gingerbread.org.uk/what-we-do/media-centre/single-parents-facts-figures (last accessed 01/2019).

state, while we live under it, it is important to draw attention to how it treats the poorest and most marginalised women.

During 2010, the Conservative-Liberal Democrat coalition government in the UK introduced a series of cuts to public spending. Studies from leading women's organisations found that, 282,000 women were out of work for more than a year as a result – the highest number since 1995. One in five mums were missing meals so their children could eat and 54.4 per cent of women suffering from domestic violence would not qualify for legal aid under the new eligibility criteria.[4] The House of Commons Library estimated that, looking at all changes to taxes and benefits from 2010–17, 86 per cent of the reduction in government spending was in spending on women.[5] But this figure does not tell the whole story. The impact of these cuts is felt particularly by low-income black women and women of colour. If austerity is a sexist policy, it is also a racist policy. In their research, Professor Akwugo Emejelu and Dr. Leah Bassel found that African and Caribbean women have an unemployment rate of 17.7 per cent, for Pakistani and Bangladeshi women it is 20.5 per cent, compared to 6.8 per cent for white women.[6]

Women of colour who are employed are more likely to be concentrated in low skilled, low paid and temporary work – regardless of their educational qualifications. These vast differences are only exacerbated by cuts, trapping these women into a cycle of poverty. Austerity locks working class, disabled and women of colour out of public life. It makes it near impossible for them to find jobs that will enable them to do more than

---

4 https://tbinternet.ohchr.org/Treaties/CEDAW/Shared%20Documents/GBR/INT_CEDAW_NGO_GBR_13333_E.pdf (last accessed 02/2019).

5 https://fullfact.org/economy/austerity-women/ (last accessed 02/2019).

6 www.plutobooks.com/blog/women-of-colours-anti-austerity-activism (last accessed 02/2019).

just survive. Freedom is one of the core principles of feminist thinking; the ability to control one's life and circumstances and be free from harm are the building blocks for any life that is worth living. Reports by the Women's Budget Group found that as a result of cuts introduced in 2010, by 2020, Black and Asian households with the lowest fifth of incomes will experience the biggest average drop in living standards of 19.2 per cent and 20.1 per cent, respectively.[7] This equates to a real-terms average annual loss in living standards of £8,407 and £11,678. We have to combat the state's logic that such devastating cuts are somehow 'necessary' to secure the economic future of the country. What good is a country that refuses to place the needs of its citizens before capitalist advancement? When feminism is hijacked by the elites and feminist discourse seeps into the upper echelons of society, it is those with power that set the feminist agenda. They distract us from the ways that the state eviscerates the lives of poor women. What use is a chamber full of 'female' politicians who declare themselves feminists if they step over dead women's bodies to do so?

The state operates in secret; often the most devastating cuts are made without public knowledge. Changes to child tax credits introduced by the Conservative government mean that from 6 April 2017 onwards, mothers will only receive tax credits for their first two children unless they can prove that subsequent children were conceived through rape.[8] 'The Rape Clause' as it is known is just one of many examples of how the government's violent programme of austerity ruins women's lives. If a woman must disclose to the state that she has been raped in order to

7   https://wbg.org.uk/blog/intersecting-inequalities-impact-austerity-bme-women-uk (last accessed 02/2019).
8   www.bbc.co.uk/news/uk-scotland-scotland-politics-39652791 (last accessed 02/2019).

receive child maintenance, her dignity, agency and power over personal information is compromised. This change was part of a wave of reforms that merged individual benefit claims into one system. 'Universal Credit' is a single payment that has been phased in over the last couple of years. It means that instead of a series of benefit payments, a single amount is paid directly into the account of the highest earner. The state's logic is that this method reduces the bureaucracy required in applying for different benefits individually, but a single payment system means that individuals receive less money over all, requiring them to re-budget their lives.

The government has repeatedly refused FOI requests into investigations over the number of claimant deaths as a result of this change. We know that thousands of disabled people have died as a direct result of government negligence surrounding Personal Independence Payments and the shift to Universal Credit has only intensified this.[9] The policy change has had devastating consequences for women's economic freedom, as women are less likely to control the family finances. The new system ensures that access to benefits is most likely controlled by male partners. Here we see how, through policy, the state can actively take power away from women and hand it to their abusers. We might argue that this is an example of the state failing; breaking its promise to protect women. But what if this was always how it was supposed to operate? These kinds of policies pull the purpose of the state into sharp relief and beg the question, what other types of violence is it hiding in plain sight?

---

9   www.parliament.uk/business/publications/written-questions-answers-statements/written-question/Commons/2018-12-19/203812 (last accessed 02/2019).

Yarl's Wood and women's detention

> Yarl's Wood IRC is a fully contained residential centre housing adult women and adult family groups awaiting immigration clearance. We focus on decency and respect in all aspects of care for our residents . . . We deliver our service based on a community model allowing residents as much freedom of movement and choice as possible.

This is the opening paragraph of the Yarl's Wood website, accompanied by images of smiling women alongside their families. Opened in 2007 by a Labour government, this centre acts as a detention facility for those awaiting deportation. Often, women can be held there for indeterminate periods of time while they fight against their removal from the country. Most if not all of the women in detention are working-class black women and women of colour seeking asylum. They are locked in, unable to leave and subjected to surveillance by outsourced security guards. Tucked away in Bedford outside of the public consciousness, it's hard to think of a more potent example of state violence. Yarl's Wood is one of eight detention centres across the country. Behind the promise of care and respect lay the horrors experienced by women in detention.

> We women here in Yarl's Wood did not anticipate our freedom would be taken from us or the impact it would have. We are on a hunger strike because we are suffering unfair imprisonment and racist abuse in this archaic institution in Britain. This is a desperate measure due to desperate circumstances. We feel voiceless, forgotten and ignored.[10]

---

10 www.newstatesman.com/politics/feminism/2018/03/message-women-yarl-s-wood-international-women-s-day (last accessed 02/2019).

This extract from a joint statement released on the 8 March 2018 by the women detained in Yarl's Wood illustrates their desperation. They used the statement to emphasise that, while celebrating women's suffrage, anyone who cares about justice should remain cognisant of the fact that women's rights are still under attack in the UK. A dossier published in 2015 by Women Against Rape and Black Women's Rape Action Project found gross sexual abuse and mistreatment in Yarl's Wood is commonplace. Women are subjected to sexual violence at the hands of guards and are often powerless to fight back. Yarl's Wood represents everything the state would like us to forget about the way it carries out its business. It is the counter-argument to a government that claims to be committed to women's rights. Yet, mainstream feminism has been curiously silent about these gross injustices. When the state enacts violence on women of colour, black women migrants especially – this silence speaks volumes. Aside from the racism inherent in mainstream feminism, one of the main reasons for this silence is that demanding an end to deportation and detention means moving beyond a liberal idea that 'protecting borders' is a reasonable concern. Mainstream feminism, infected by a neo-liberal policy agenda, does not possess the political will or the capacity to make such demands.

State killings

Dorothy Groce was shot and paralysed by police as they searched for another suspect in 1985. Cynthia Jarrett died from heart failure during a police search of her home in 1985. In 1993, Joy Gardner died after police descended on her house and restrained her until she stopped breathing. They had come to deport her back to the West Indies because her visa had lapsed. Sarah Reed died on 11 January 2016 from 'self-strangulation' in Holloway

Prison, after prison guards and psychiatric nurses ignored her deteriorating mental state. In 2017, Annabella Landsberg died in a segregation cell in HMP Peterborough after being left there for 21 hours. She was diabetic and suffered from physical and mental health problems. The list reaches far back in time and will continue into the future as long as our politics does nothing to oppose the most violent elements of the state. These are just a few examples of state killings that occurred as a result of coming into contact with police or the prison system, and they reveal a pattern. All were black women.

In the liberal feminist rationale, the police and prisons are necessary because they protect women from danger. They are necessary because without them, society would descend into chaos. But is the world not already chaotic for the black people who die in custody or are deported in the dead of night? It is not already a dystopian nightmare for the undocumented migrants and the women and their families who burned to death in Grenfell tower as a direct result of state negligence? Or those unjustly deported to their deaths in the Windrush Scandal?

If black women die disproportionately at the hands of the police, historically and in the present moment, we must ask, what is the purpose of the police and detention system? Is it right that *some* women must die so that others are protected? Do we wish to be the recipients of that kind of protection? When we understand race and gender as inseparable, there is no feminist case for the existence of the police. The police are deployed to do the state's bidding and are enmeshed in the oppressive consequences of this task. This is why, despite liberal feminism's insistence, increased numbers of women entering the police force can never transform its practice. State killings act as another mechanism to remove women from public life. The state expresses itself through the use of violence, it then rationa-

31

lises women's deaths through 'inquest' and apology. Coming to terms with this can shake the very foundation of what we have been taught about police and the court system being vehicles for justice. But what might a feminist response to state violence look like and why is it important to craft one?

A feminist response

In her book, *Lean Out*, Dawn Foster argues:

> The women on the frontline of the new feminist campaigning accept that capitalism and the political and the power elites are no friend to women, and that to have a stab at life that can support you and your children, the answer isn't to internalise the hatred society casts your way, but to fight to reveal injustice and refuse to participate.[11]

This refusal to participate takes many forms: feminist activists are finding new and creative ways to oppose austerity. Their activism is driven by the human consequences of cuts to services, prison expansion and state violence.

Another world is possible. Austerity has created a dire situation that requires an urgent response. Feminist thinking has helped provide one that is strategic, focused and powerful. One of the clearest examples of this is Sisters Uncut, a feminist direct action group that emerged from the 2014–15 anti-austerity movements. They challenged these movements, arguing that the issues of women and non-binary people were left out of their analysis, and that a specific focus on domestic and sexual violence should be at the core of any critique of the state. Sisters

11   Dawn Foster, *Lean Out* (London: Repeater Books, 2015), p. 78.

Uncut has put domestic and sexual violence on the national agenda through consistent disruption, focused campaigning and the strong symbolism embedded in their protests. They use subvertising adverts to draw attention to the gutting of vital services across the city. In 2018, they gained press attention for storming the BAFTA'S red carpet to tell Theresa May #TimesUp on her attempt to further criminalise survivors through the Domestic Violence Bill. Sisters and Siblings across the country organise in regional networks highlighting the ways we can use feminism to fight back.

When I ask Sandy where the idea to create Sisters came from, she tells me:

> The first thing we did was recognise our conditions, we asked what the fuck is happening around us? Who is in power and what are they doing with it? . . . Sisters was a feminist response to that, a feminist response to austerity – we were born from a resistance to cuts. We have a lot of different focuses, there are people who are interested in the state, there are people who want to focus on transformative justice and think beyond it. We say it's important to think in, against and beyond the state.

And who or what is their feminist response inspired by?

> It's heavily influenced by the activists that have inspired us like Angela Davis, Assata Shakur, Audre Lorde, Olive Morris . . . I think our work comes from a feminist understanding of care, it comes from an understanding that gender oppression is fundamentally linked to wider exploitation of all people that happens in society. Exploitation that is enabled by cuts to vital services. Uprooting subordination means re-thinking the

ways we relate to one another. Our feminist work allows us to bring the concerns of domestic workers and migrant workers to the fore and give them the platform to speak for themselves. When we recognise the links between cuts, exploitation and gender, we create the possibility for deep, deep links of solidarity with people who are radically different from us. Using feminism as a base for our work allows us to change, think and adapt and ensure that our focus isn't singular.

Sandy sees direct action as a rehearsal for the revolution. It's a trial run, a way of enacting the kind of future you hope to build:

Direct action allows us to take the fight to the streets, where the people are and out of the hands of the ruling class. If people can see it, they can imagine it. Direct action is a physical act that should be designed so that the story tells its self. It seeks to change power dynamics directly, rather than relying on others to make changes for us. We must be creative and flexible in the way we use direct action. We also recognise the ways that community organising can be utilised to help us imagine things that don't yet seem possible.

There are no easy answers. When we first become aware of state violence, it can be overwhelming, disheartening and impossible to think of alternatives. But feminist responses like this should bring us hope. Neo-liberalism asks us to trust the state and turn our back on those who are dispossessed by it. Collective organising is one antidote to state violence because it requires us to work together towards common interests, an idea that is entirely antithetical to the individualism that underpins neo-liberal thinking. Collective responses remind us that as much as it benefits the state to delink and isolate us, we need each other to survive. In order to build a world that is worth living, we need to face up to the realities of the state's actions. Starting with changes in local communities – defending shelters, youth centres, organising against gentrification – helps lay the groundwork for making cross-country and eventual transnational demands. A commitment to disrupting the state's violence when and where we see it takes feminism outside of the realm of words and theories and makes it a living, breathing set of principles. It reminds us that where we can make interventions, we should and that only work that seeks to shake and unsettle the very foundations of the sexist state is feminist work.

Chapter 3

The fight for reproductive justice[1]

So that just as to assure elimination of economic classes requires the revolt of the underclass (the proletariat) . . . so to assure the elimination of sexual classes requires the revolt of the underclass (women) and the seizure of control of reproduction: not only the full restoration to women of ownership of their own bodies, but also their (temporary) seizure of control of human fertility – the new population biology as well as all the social institutions of childbearing and childrearing. – Shulamith Firestone

On Friday 25 May 2018, Ireland repealed the 8th Amendment, a part of the constitution that equated the life of an unborn foetus with the person carrying it, making abortion legal only in cases where that person's life was deemed to be at risk. This amendment was introduced by a referendum in September 1983, which asked the electorate to insert the pro-life article into an already deeply conservative constitution.

---

1 The fights for reproductive rights I outline in this chapter were historically based in the women's rights movement, but abortion and reproductive justice are not exclusively a 'women's issue' and the language of these movements is historically circumstantial.

Abortion and bodily autonomy have always been a focal point of feminist concern. In the seventies, Marxist feminists like Shulamith Firestone argued that because the family was linked to biology, women's liberation depended on seizing control of reproductive technologies. Critical feminists have long believed that every person should have the right to bodily autonomy and that increased control over one's body means more control over one's fate. The call for 'Free, Safe and Legal' abortion was a radical call for a transformative public health system that placed the rights of women first, and a core demand of mainstream movements in the 1960s and 1970s, largely comprised of white middle class women. Abortion was partly decriminalised in England and Wales in 1967 through a Private Members Bill; the act made abortion legal up until 28 weeks in all grounds of Great Britain except Northern Ireland. When this law was passed, a number of legal challenges emerged that sought to limit the kinds of doctors who could perform an abortion and the permissions needed to access one. In 1975, the National Abortion Campaign was established with the aim of protecting this crucial legal right. The NAC worked closely with grassroots feminist outlets like Spare Rib to protect against legal challenges to the right to access abortion. They crafted progressive abortion legislation, which sought to improve access to healthcare and ultimately, make the process of accessing abortion less traumatic.

My body, my choice

Choice rhetoric was the foundation of feminist campaigns for the legal right to abortion. It was thought that enshrining the right to abortion in law would secure it forever. In this way, legal frameworks shaped the priorities of the mainstream feminist movement. Feminists fought for abortion using a top down approach; the logic being that if the law changed, so would society. But as well as failing to acknowledge the limits of the law, this approach failed to consider reproduction from a structural perspective or examine how reproductive labour is a key component of social reproduction. 'Social reproduction' refers to a broad set of theories that argue that the production of goods and services are inseparable from the production of life. It examines the way that racialised, gendered reproductive labour (things like childcare and housework) is key to the production of capital. The right to bodily autonomy is important not only because of what it means for the individual, but because women having greater control over their own reproduction has the potential to transform how work is distributed in and outside of the home.

Choice rhetoric pushes for legislative enshrinement of reproductive rights. But, in an oppressive society not all legal rights over one's body are created equal. Wealthy white women have always been able to exercise greater agency over their reproductive capacity because they can afford private healthcare and specialist medical advice. Poorer women, most likely women of colour, have the least control over their reproductive fates. The law cannot address the conditions that create these disparities. While the law seems the most obvious way to draw attention to women's lack of control over their reproductive futures, it cannot be the only way that we think about reproduction. The law is no arbiter of fairness nor it is a guarantee for justice.

Before the state made abortions legal, women performed and received backstreet abortions, advised each other on contraception, shared knowledge and resources for those in desperate situations. These underground links were particularly strong in places like Northern Ireland, a place with some of the most stringent abortion legislation in Europe. Radical feminists have always responded to the gravity of situations placed before them without the state's stamp of approval.

Rights versus justice

The difference between radical and mainstream feminist movements is the ability to recognise the context in which demands for freedom and autonomy are made. As the women's movement strengthened in the US and UK, a clear divide emerged between those interested in reproductive rights and reproductive justice. In her seminal text, *Women, Race and Class*, Angela Davis examined the mainstream feminist demand for abortion by tracing the eugenicist origins of the family planning movement and mass sterilisation of black women and indigenous communities by the federal government in the US: 'The abortion rights activists of the early 1970s should have examined the history of their movement. Had they done so, they might have understood why so many of their Black sisters adopted a posture of suspicion toward their cause.'[2] Margaret Sanger, reproductive rights advocate responsible for the first birth control-clinic in the United States was a vocal eugenicist and advocated population control for those deemed 'unfit' (physically disabled women, black and poor women).[3] Davis noted that black women's scepticism of the abortion rights movement was linked to mainstream feminism's failure to recognise the racist origins of the demand for abortion, and respond to the alarming rates at which black women were dying from illegal abortions due to inadequate healthcare. The term 'Reproductive Justice' was coined by twelve black women at a pro-choice conference in Chicago in 1994. Loretta J. Ross

2   Angela Davis, *Women, Race and Class* (New York: Vintage Books, 1983), p. 261.
3   https://isreview.org/issue/91/black-feminism-and-intersectionality (last accessed 02/ 2019).

writes: 'We created "reproductive justice" because we believed that true health care for women needed to include a full range of reproductive health services. While abortion is one primary health issue, we knew that abortion advocacy alone inadequately addressed the intersectional oppressions of white supremacy, misogyny, and neo-liberalism.'[4] Many grassroots black feminist organising groups across the UK and US, such as SisterSong, a Chicago based feminist collective, and OWAAD, who campaigned against the unsafe administering of contraceptive drug Depo provera in working class black and brown communities in the UK, adopted an approach in line with these values before the term had been coined. They expanded the scope of the abortion debate. They wanted justice, not rights. They wanted to create the conditions for liberation by enabling women control over reproductive technologies and creating dignified, healthy and sustainable communities for them to raise their children in.

Reproductive Justice advocates recognised that rights can be revoked as easily as they can be granted and focusing solely on the 'right' to have an abortion obscured the many other determining factors around childbirth, child-rearing and family. It absolved the state of its responsibilities to create the support mechanisms for raising families. If the decision to have a child is simply a woman's 'choice', the responsibility for the well-being of children is shifted onto mothers instead of the society in which children are raised. Women can be blamed for their bad 'choices'; single mothers with multiple children become the target for policy makers who view them as a scourge on society. Sexist logics are reaffirmed.

Reproductive Justice looks at the issue of reproduction holistically, encompassing the barriers that create disparities in family

---

4   Loretta J. Ross, 'Reproductive Justice as Intersectional Feminist Activism', *Souls* 19, no. 3, (2017): 286–314.

planning. As an approach, it demands a universal free health-care, living wage, programs that give agency to parents who are drug users. It recognises that the way we live directly influences the 'choices' we make. It examines the ways that eugenics has shaped our notion of family and forces feminists to think about the racist logic of 'population control' that birthed the desire for contraceptives and its long-lasting impact on medical care today. It recognises the many ways that healthcare systems deny transgender people access to basic reproductive technologies through surgical sterilisation and restricting access to fertility preservation. A number of European countries such as Finland, Switzerland and Greece require sterilisation to undergo medical transition. Although this is not the case in the UK, there is no publicly funded access to gamete storage, meaning that it is near impossible for poorer trans people to save their reproductive cells. A reproductive justice approach realises that *mother does not equal cis woman* and incorporates the complex ways that parenthood can manifest into a liberatory political framework. It implores us to raise our children together, and recognise the responsibility we have to secure each other's health and happiness by building a just world. The conditions that shape the way we live – capitalism, racism, sexism – are entirely beyond an individual's control. In a world defined by these structures, 'choice' and true freedom will continue to elude us unless we fight to transform the way our societies function.

Reproductive justice in Ireland

The history of debates about abortion in Ireland is fraught with historic examples of abuse of power by the church and state, which transformed abortion into the country's dirty little secret. Ireland's conservatism on reproductive issues exists partly because of an alliance between conservative lawmakers and the church, which sought to enshrine the values of heterosexual marriage and family into the constitution. Access to abortion was deemed a threat to the stability of the nuclear family life – and indeed it is. If the nuclear family is a vehicle for the regulation of women's sexuality, desire and the basis for the exploitation of their labour, then it has always been in the state's interest to control how, when and under what conditions family life can exist.

Irish broadcaster, RTE's exit poll suggested that 72.1 per cent of women and 87.6 per cent of 18–24 year olds intended to vote YES for Repeal on the day of the historic referendum. The referendum drew the third highest turnout ever, with YES achieving 66.4 per cent of the vote, a majority of 706,349.[5] Grassroots feminist mobilisation was key in securing the votes of young people and most crucially, gaining the swing votes that led to the landslide. This is a clear example of the potential for feminists to spread influence, mobilise and win on an issue through collective organising. However, it does reveal the core differences between rights-based and justice-based approaches to securing reproductive freedom. The referendum was won by a collaboration between younger and older women, who flew home, knocked on doors, convinced their brothers and husbands and sons to vote YES. For many adult women who had lived their lives under this regime, been in receipt of backstreet abortions, traded illegal pills and other methods of aborting in private, this was a seminal moment. But feminists on the ground warned that a change in the law would not automatically equal control over reproductive futures.

---

5   www.theguardian.com/world/2018/may/26/ireland-votes-by-landslide-to-legalise-abortion (last accessed 02/2019).

Rachel Watters, NUS Women's Officer and reproductive justice activist has seen this first hand:

> The law cannot take you all the way; we're seeing that now. The new law has come into effect but it's already clear that hospitals are going to interpret the 12-week gestational limit conservatively in order to protect themselves. Although you can invest all of this hope in the law changing things, it's not necessarily going to happen. There have been grassroots activists on the ground pointing this out from the very beginning . . . The divide between reproductive rights groups and reproductive justice came down to an idea that for the sake of the campaign, we have to compromise our more radical ideals to sell this to middle Ireland . . . There were a lot of suppressed tensions during the campaign, we knew we all had different objectives after the referendum, after the legislation but understood that we needed a YES vote . . . it was an uneasy coalition for several months.

This tension highlights that there was no 'singular' feminist movement fighting for bodily autonomy. Different groups with conflicting visions for the future worked together because they realised that they could collaborate, share resources and coordinate their organising efforts. But 'coming together' in this context meant trying to persuade the public that they were ready for a more progressive abortion policy. *Persuasion* will never equal justice. This 'united voice' betrayed many women who did not fit into an easily recognisable template for the sake of the argument. Rachel tells me:

> There was this idea that you couldn't really compromise what was going on by asking mainstream groups to focus on the

cases that were 'less easy to sympathise with' . . . women of colour were not approached to speak of their own experiences. The assumption was, 'we need a Dublin organisation that we already know the face of to speak for you'.

When Ireland is coded 'white', and 'Irish woman' means only those who fall under that coding, large swathes of the population are erased and indeed, actively silenced. To the movement they represent a complication, a step too far. But nobody understands the stakes around the right to access abortion and reproductive justice more than working class women, women of colour and migrant women for whom, abortion is about more than religion or stigma or shame; it means life or death.

Nameless faces

Two of the main stories mobilised by the joint coalition campaigning for a YES vote were that of Savita Halappanavar and Miss Y. Savita died in 2012 at University Hospital in Galway from complications from a septic miscarriage after she was denied an abortion by the Irish state. Miss Y is an asylum seeker and rape survivor who arrived in Ireland and became suicidal after realising she was pregnant. She was forced to carry her baby to full term. Although individuals were given the right to travel abroad to access abortion in 1992, Savita's case reaffirmed the devastating reality for the need for uncomplicated access to abortion in Ireland. Her symbol helped reignite appetite for debate and helped women's organisations place greater pressure on the Irish government to respond to the crisis in healthcare for Irish women.

According to MBRRACE-UK, Black women are five times more likely to die from complications during pregnancy than their white counterparts.[6] Grassroots reproductive justice groups based in Ireland such as MERJ (Migrant and Ethnic Minorities for Reproductive Justice) have consistently fought to broaden the focus of the debate beyond abortion towards the conditions that make reproduction possible. They told me what reproductive justice means to them:

> MERJ sees reproductive justice in a broader spatial context, we see reproductive justice as the right to a home, fair, equal and non exploitative paid labour, access to affordable child-care, to live free from domestic violence, gender violence or any violence and free access to healthcare to all people. We consider reproductive justice to be an all-encompassing term for bodily autonomy. To have reproductive justice means to be the sole director of your body.

As a group of migrant women, they speak for themselves with the intention of drawing attention to the glaring holes in abortion rights discourse:

> It is resolutely clear that minoritised voices were effectively silenced during the campaign. It is quite obvious how white and middle class the campaign was. The decision to exclude migrants and ethnic minorities from the campaign has proven to be a big mistake and a possible step backwards for the left.

While the images and stories of Miss Y. and Savita were used to create empathy, living women who looked like them were actively erased from the mainstream debate. It is no coincidence that two of the most high-profile cases mobilised by abortion

---

6   www.npeu.ox.ac.uk/downloads/files/mbrrace-uk/reports/MBRRACE-UK%20 Maternal%20Report%202018%20-%20Web%20Version.pdf (last accessed 02/2019).

rights activists involved women of colour. Women of colour become hyper visible only at the point where their bodies are incapacitated. They are easily turned into symbols when they are grieving, suffering, or dead. For MERJ, the fight for reproductive justice means abolishing the harmful legislative and institutional structures that were designed to restrict bodily autonomy:

> The abolishment of sexist, racist and misogynistic constitutions and legislations that have been put in place by the government is one of the main driving forces behind our fight for the right to abortion, among many other things in Ireland. We need to disrupt these systems before we can begin to build a society that would be safe and just for all women.

Through political education and protest, MERJ have highlighted the number of migrant women in Direct Provision centres who would have limited access to abortion and who die in silence, as the world looks the other way. They refused to stop drawing attention to the fact that 40 per cent of maternity deaths in Ireland involve migrant women, despite them making up a fraction of the population. For migrants in detention, the right to an abortion will never be a choice they can freely exercise.

The call for a radical approach to reproductive autonomy is also a call to end detention and fight for free and publicly accessible healthcare. For MERJ and other grassroots organisers, Repealing the 8th was only the first step in a long and complicated journey towards reproductive freedom. For every movement's success, there are countless nameless women whose stories are used as a tool for mobilisation. Savita's death and the story of Miss Y became tragedies, *after the fact,* but would the mainstream abortion rights movement, with its narrow framing, have saved them? If we view the clawing back of rights as our only goal (and there are many immediate reasons why we must) we risk reducing the possibility to ask new and exciting questions about how we might transform modes of reproduction.

Reproductive futures

In July 2019, English MPs voted 332 votes to 99 to change Northern Ireland's abortion law if devolution was not restored at Stormont by October 2019. This means that Abortion in Northern Ireland has only recently been decriminalised, the possibility of persecution has been lifted from those administering and undergoing abortions. The tendency to consider the UK a progressive environment for reproductive justice sorely underestimates the number of people, who despite the change in law may still have no recourse to abortion services due to geographical location, immigration status, conscientious objections from medical professionals and a lack of medical infrastructure. Legality does not equal access. There are many more complicated demands to be made: mainstream movements will always defeat their own purpose as long as they consider the law as the sole indicator of progress. Perhaps the most powerful thing that can be done is sabotaging the law-making project and refusing to concede that abortion is unlawful. As feminists, we must continue breaking the law to provide abortions and associated medications on demand in order to live the lives we deserve. Those who have been cast outside of the 'acceptable' face of abortion rights should be at the centre of our demands. By embracing complication, we stand a chance of getting beyond the rhetoric of the individual, towards a future in which the state no longer regulates our bodies and we instead can craft a kind of reproduction that exists in the common interest.

Ireland represents a microcosm of the kinds of shifts that are possible in countries across the world. While being strategic is necessary for any feminist project, we need to think, as Sophie Lewis argues, about how to win *radically*. Mainstream abortion rights debates often involve making concessions in the way we speak about abortion in the public eye. Some individuals become more deserving of abortion than others. But in her work on feminist family abolition,[7] Lewis makes the necessary case that abortion is an acceptable form of killing as a means of enabling people to stop doing unwanted gestational work. She argues that we need to remove the shame in the way we talk about acceptable forms of killing because anyone who is tasked with this decision understands the stakes. Winning radically would mean envisioning futures where parenting could be done in 'queerer, more comradely ways,'[8] where mothering is not exclusive to mothers, a world where abortion is provided on demand, a world without work.

The popular slogan 'Free, Safe, Legal' does not begin to approach what could be possible. In the current landscape, when our rights continue to be put to public vote, the very least we can do is stand firm in our demands for reproductive justice. Our movements must focus on migrants in direct provision and working class people who cannot afford to travel, standing with those who demand abortions beyond prescribed gestational limits. Our feminism must begin with a refusal to trust that the language of rights can take us all the way.

---

7 www.youtube.com/watch?v=jMGptJXz618&t=47s (last accessed 02/2019).
8 Sophie Lewis, *Full Surrogacy Now: Feminism Against Family* (London: Verso, 2019).

Chapter 4

Transmisogyny: Who wins?

When I say trans, I also mean escape. I mean choice. I mean autonomy. I mean wanting something greater than what you told me. Wanting more possibilities than the one you forced on me. – Travis Alabanza

Anyone who's been deemed 'unnatural' in the face of reigning biological norms, anyone who's experienced injustices wrought in the name of natural order, will realise that the glorification of 'nature' has nothing to offer us – the queer and trans among us, the differently-abled, as well as those who have suffered discrimination due to pregnancy or duties connected to child-rearing . . . If nature is unjust, change nature! – Laboria Cuboniks

For Naomi Hersi.

It begins with a cry. In the delivery room, newborns are assigned a sex according to their genitals. Everything from science, to culture, to common wisdom affirms to us that there are only two options to choose from: male and female. These categories refer to our 'biological makeup'. To deviate from either option is unnatural and to 'journey' from one to another is sacrilege. Because our society sees sex as 'natural', and therefore self-evident, it has become unquestionable. It is hard to recognise that this process of assignment and categorisation is something human beings have created to make the world intelligible. If there are only two categories, it is easier for us to organise the world and attach feelings, emotions and ways of being to each one. Those feelings, emotions and ways of being are commonly referred to as 'gender'. There is no way to adequately describe what gender is. Every definition does a disservice to the shifting, multiple and complex set of power relations that come to shape a person's gender. But loosely, feminists have understood gender as our sense of self in the world, how we present our bodies, speak, move – anything that refers to our presentation and relationship to our own bodies. This presentation is shaped by the male/female categorisation. The idea is that if sex refers to biology, gender refers to the social roles that are ascribed on the basis of sex.

Bodies

Feminists have rightly been concerned with the process of sex assignment: they recognise that throughout history, to be 'female' has often meant death, mutilation and oppression. Sex categorisation has been the starting point for well-known feminist theories. But the idea of sex as immutable became a focal point of radical, lesbian feminism in the West, and more specifically, America during the 70s and 80s. This was not the case across the board, especially among black feminists, but there are many notable instances of feminist organising that were hostile towards trans women during this time. The publication of Janice Raymond's *Transsexual Empire* in 1979 marked a turning point for the development of arguments against trans life in America. Raymond's argument relied, at least in part, on the importance of biology in forming women's bodily integrity. 'Transsexualism' as she called it, not only reaffirmed gender stereotypes, but was a violation of 'harmony – wholeness, be-ing.'[1] Though disguised, the credence given to biology in these arguments affirmed the idea that women are *born*, and not *made* or *named*; that there is something inherent in biology that is crucial to womanhood.

This idea is inextricably linked with gender essentialism – the notion that there is a fixed and universal essence present in men and women and that we possess different innate qualities. This logic helped support arguments that rooted women's oppression and men's dominance in the body. Bodily approaches from many radical lesbian thinkers saw heterosexual sex as a battleground – 'use and abuse' as referred to by Andrea Dworkin – and the area where male dominance was exerted using genitalia. During the 1970s and 80s, women's oppression was analysed exclusively by some feminists, through the lens of sex and sexuality. They argued that sex work and pornography put women in subordinate positions, and were akin to violation. This way of viewing women, their bodies and their relations with men was central to a number of high-profile Western feminist disputes. The most notable example is the pornography wars of the 1990s between anti-porn feminists who argued that pornography subjugated women and exploited their bodies, and pro-sex feminists who argued that pornography provided some possibility for agency in women's expression of sexuality.

Is sex real?

There are a number of scientific studies that point to the fact that human beings' sexual biology is far more varied than we

1   Janice Raymond, *Transsexual Empire* (New York: Teachers College Press, 1994), p. 18.

give it credit for.[2] The existence of people who are born defying sex determination systems proves this. Many intersex infants, individuals born with variations in 'male' and 'female' sex characteristics, are assigned a sex at birth and often have surgery to 'correct' their genitalia without their consent. This demonstrates the power of sex as a classification system that makes us intelligible; we do not live in a society that knows what to do with bodies that do not conform to rigid binaries. In some instances, doctors can choose the sex of an infant, revealing the absurdity of the idea that sex is first and foremost, biological. The fight for intersex people's rights to bodily autonomy and recognition is not the same fight as transgender people's (though the two overlap often as many intersex people are trans). But they are both fights against a rigid and violent system of sexual essentialism that renders many bodies and lives incomprehensible, forcing conformity and/or expulsion of those deemed unruly.

Judith Butler broke new ground in 1990 with her seminal text, *Gender Trouble*. In it she suggested that there is nothing natural about 'biological sex'. She argued that sex is a construction just like gender and that sex becomes gender because of how we talk about it and how it is practiced through a series of performative repetitions. Sex *is* gender and the way we think about both is entirely social. If one group of people consistently behave, speak, move, present themselves in one way and another in the 'opposite' way, we reaffirm the idea that there is actually an inherent difference between those two groups when no such difference exists. While male and female bodies may have different physical capabilities in particular contexts, these differences in regards to testosterone and oestrogen are not only exagger-

2   https://blogs.scientificamerican.com/voices/stop-using-phony-science-to-justify-transphobia (last accessed 09/2019).

ated,[3] there is also a whole range of variations across members of the opposite sex. Many women are physically stronger than men; many men are physically weaker than women. These are not exceptions that defy a rule; there simply is no rule. 'Biological' differences are often exaggerated to explain phenomena that are entirely unconnected: personality, social and political interests, cognitive ability. To argue that there is a clear difference between sex and gender serves to solidify the idea that biological sex, prior to human beings inventing it and naming its tenants, exists.

To say that gender and sex are social constructions is not to say that they are unimportant or that gender is as simple as putting on a different hat each day. Butler is often misquoted as claiming gender is a 'performance' when instead she argues it might be better to view it as a ritual that is made up of certain kinds of repetitive behaviours that sediment over time.[4] When we repeat this behaviour, we create ourselves. Because of the way it organises our lives, gender has life or death consequences. Consider the way that anyone who does not conform to ideas of their assigned sex is heavily policed. Butch women. Feminine men. Transgender men and women, non-binary people and anyone who is gender non-conforming. Daily, people die because they challenge, subvert and threaten the visual script dictated by the gender binary. In the Americas, 80 per cent of the trans women killed as a result of gendered violence are 35 years of age or younger.[5] Gender harms us all

3   https://thepsychologist.bps.org.uk/volume-30/october-2017/testosterone-key-sex-differences-human-behaviour?fbclid=IwAR2fL3iL1if5CgoynLbjwmo9Ahm8Bq-UgYbJLK-TmwQfueRy9fbWV6oHacs (last accessed 10/2019).

4   Judith Butler, *Gender Trouble* (London: Routledge, 1999), p. 178.

5   www.oas.org/en/iachr/lgtbi/docs/Annex-Registry-Violence-LGBTI.pdf (last accessed 10/2019).

when it is used as a vehicle for violence and exploitation. But when feminists adopt a binary understanding of gender and an essentialist idea that biology is destiny, they put trans women at risk.

Understanding that there is nothing 'natural' or 'stable' about human biology helps us dismantle the idea that women's oppression is rooted in a singular place. We can believe that sex and gender are made up categories, embellished by social attitudes and recognise that the violence that occurs as a result of them is very real. It is the violence that defines our experience of the world, not our biological makeup that we often know little about it. (How often do you think about your chromosomes?) Often being *perceived* as a woman or failing to do womanhood correctly is enough to put somebody at risk of harm. It is also important to remember that Western conceptions of gender are not and have never been, universal. Gender has no single story. There are countless examples of gender non-conforming and variant expressions across the world that challenge the idea of 'man' and woman' and evidence that they have existed for centuries. The colonial project played a large part in marking certain sexual and gender practice taboos, in line with religious and imperialist ideas of nature. A number of colonial projects used penal law to outlaw expressions of gender variance and 'homosexual' acts between men in places such as India, Kenya, Australia and Uganda. This is not to imply that non-Western examples of gender variance were always free from policing and scrutiny in pre-colonial contexts, but to reaffirm that though gender may appear self-evident, its history is dependent on context. Just because specific ideas and practices of gender are central in the West, does not make them a global phenomenon.

Generational divides: TERFS

Our media is full of scaremongering about Generation Z and their obsession with sexual and gender fluidity. A number of celebrities like Sam Smith, Amandla Stenberg and Indya Moore have expressed a rejection of or ambivalence about the sex they were assigned at birth and being fixed in a gender binary, opting to use they/them pronouns. Gender fluidity presents a threat to the stable ideas of gender and sexuality. This seems so threatening because compliance to a system of categorisation within stable sexual categories also means compliance to the unjust system of governance that dictates it. Refusing binaries means challenging the harmful systems that keep them in place and make our lives miserable by dictating what we can and cannot do. Refusing the world as it is also means refusing racism, capitalism and a whole host of associated violences. This is threatening to liberal feminism, but there is a silver lining to the chaos created by these generational divides in approaches to gender. Feminists can speak back and more importantly, organise against oppressive structures like sexism on a local and global scale, by unsettling the idea that binaries define us. Chaos allows us to look at the way that violence is a central organising principle for our societies and more importantly, helps us identify the bodies that are nearest to it.

The pressure to 'do' gender correctly is so embedded in our social lives that it is hard to conceive of a world without it. Coming to the realisation that everything you have been told about the fixed nature of your own body is a lie can shake you to your core. There is a kind of feminism that thrives off the anxiety caused by this realisation. Trans Exclusionary Radical Feminists (TERFs) or those who call themselves 'gender-critical' use a specific feminist logic to locate the source of women's oppression in biology. For them, sex is a fixed category that cannot be changed. While many young feminists espouse TERF ideology, the public face of TERF organising is often older liberal white and middle class women who vocalise 'concerns' about the inclusion of trans women in feminist spaces and women's rights discourse, lamenting the 'generational divides' in feminist thinking. They view the changing nature of language to describe gender and sexuality as a threat to feminist advancement, tending to be dismissive of newer kinds of feminist practice that take a radically materialist and intersectional approach as their starting point. They use these concerns to foster a 'trans panic!': a manufactured fear that newer feminist movements erase cis women's sex-based oppression, undermining the structural nature of misogyny and pushing more people to medically transition.

Popular TERF arguments in the public eye centre on the safety of children. Perhaps one of the most insidious is the idea that young children, who are grappling with gender, are being pushed into early transition. The logic holds that young women (especially butch lesbians and those who are gender non-conforming) are being given an easy way to 'opt out' of womanhood or lesbianism because of societal pressure to become trans men. Straight women attached to TERF Ideology have attempted to disguise themselves as 'allies' to the queer community, arguing that lesbians are disappearing. Their logic holds that any young woman who feels trapped by gender expectations or thinks critically about gender would opt to transition. But this argument assumes that to be trans means to move from one binary gender to another. This is not only incorrect; it simplifies the complex and deeply personal relationship to gender and presentation that many trans people have. Some opt for medical transition, some don't, some grapple with their bodies as they appear, and others do not. It becomes easier to argue against transness when a simple narrative about what it means to be trans is presented and dissected. In the UK, children do not have access to medical transition, yet the scaremongering tactics that TERFS employ rely heavily on ideas of young children's proximity to underground sex confirmation surgery.

Under our current systems, those experiencing gender dysphoria cannot easily access medical transition. There are a number of exhaustive and pathologising processes that one must undertake before medical transition even becomes an option, such as being required to recount childhood trauma and being assessed by a panel of medical gatekeepers who determine your viability for transition. What TERFs miss in their attempt to manufacture a moral panic about transgender people is that feminist thinking enables cis women to despise the social consequences of the sex we are assigned at birth and still comfortably occupy a gender that 'corresponds' with it. To assume individuals' transition flippantly suggests that medical transition is an easily available unnecessary luxury, when in reality, it can often be one of the only routes to safety for trans people whose bodies have been deemed 'unruly' by society. Medical transition saves lives in a world where gender scripts mean the difference between life and death. But perhaps most urgently, we must ask ourselves, *what is wrong with increased access to medical transition?* TERFS characterise being transgender as a societal failure. No amount of refutation, 'rational' argumentation, scientific case studies or statistics can undo a way of thinking that seeks to render trans life impossible. Instead of arguing on the terms of TERFs who are increasingly setting the tone on public debates, as young feminists we must draw attention to the devastating, real world consequences of discursive attacks on trans people, trans women especially. The 'gender-critical' movement is strategic and organised – at the core; TERFS are not concerned with the welfare of children or adults, but simply finding sympathetic vehicles through which to promote their antagonism towards trans life.

TERFS have been mobilising across the country, using the internet to organise. Popular online forums like Mumsnet and Reddit are home to pages and pages dedicated to co-ordinating hate campaigns targeting trans people. Hannah Woodhead argues that 'Mumsnet has become a breeding ground for trans-phobic voices; a space where they can laugh about sabotaging an NHS survey aimed at LGBTQ+ users and scorn trans participa-tion in sport, or ponder that trans rights are a millennial issue.'[6] Claims that young children are being pushed into transition without a choice are reminiscent of homophobic campaigners and legislators who mobilised the idea of protecting innocent children from 'homosexuals', leading to legislation like Section 28 in the UK, enacted in 1988. The aim is to legislate queerness, transness, anything that upsets the binary out of existence. Race and class play a key part in the authority of the anti-trans lobby. It is no coincidence that the most vocal and prominent TERFs in the UK tend to be middle class white women. Their reliance on biological essentialism reveals much about their conceptual-isations of race. They rely on the power of essentialism because they see how successfully it functions as an organising prin-ciple for society.

There are ideological links between biological essentialism and scientific racism: both see the body in absolute terms. Many prominent TERFS and their allies have aligned themselves with members of the alt-right. Well-known British feminists have appeared in YouTube videos hosted by men spreading alt-right,

6   www.huckmag.com/perspectives/opinion-perspectives/mumsnet-transphobia-online (last accessed 01/2019).

fascistic ideology in the art world.[7] In the US, the 'Women's Liberation Front' colluded with conservative and religious groups to defend the rights of employers to fire transgender staff.[8] Those who rely on this kind of thinking are also the least likely to adopt an intersectional approach to feminist practice. These 'feminists' are not concerned with changing the material conditions of women's lives so that subjugation and exploitation are no longer necessary parts of it. Instead, they direct their anxieties about the kinds of violence that all women experience in a patriarchal society towards trans women so that cis women become 'oppressed' by the existence of trans women or by expansive ideas of gender. Essentialist understandings offer a simple truth about ourselves that is easy to swallow. Pathologising trans people makes it easier to blame them for societal ills and to pit cis and trans women's issues against one another. This merely distracts us from the most pressing issues at hand.

If gender is not a fixed, immovable truth, then everything we know about ourselves as women is at risk of collapsing. Recent debates around the reform of the Gender Recognition Act 2004, a piece of legislation that created a process that enables individuals to change their legal gender, demonstrates the manifestation of this anxiety. Large groups of 'gender-critical' feminists encouraged others to sabotage the government's attempt to make the process of obtaining a Gender Recognition Certificate easier by registering their objection to trans women entering women only spaces. Despite the fact that The Equality Act 2014 already enshrines this right in law, the mobilisation around this particular point betrays the TERF obsession with genitalia and the penis as a symbol of violence. TERF ideology

---

7 www.thewhitepube.co.uk/on-trauma (last accessed 09/2019).

8 www.vox.com/identities/2019/9/5/20840101/terfs-radical-feminists-gender-critical (last accessed 09/2019).

also hurts men: if violence is inherent to certain kinds of genitalia, then as feminists, we leave little space for fostering the transformative gender relations necessary for a liberated future. Men are not inherently bad and women are not inherently good but the idea that one cannot escape their own biology traps us all in the oppressor/oppressed binary with no hope of abolishing it.

Under the guise of 'protecting women', TERF movements seek to re-establish strict gender codes. Whether through policing public bathrooms or making access to medical transition harder than it should be, they align themselves with the church and the state (who are not natural allies to feminists) in order to legitimise their agenda. By reoccupying the role of victim, cisgender women are able to frame themselves as the recipients of a kind of onslaught from a group of people that make up less than 1 per cent of the population. Concerns of 'female erasure' are central to TERF arguments, but what is most frightening, is the way they have successfully merged transphobia with right-wing rhetoric about threats to freedom of speech and the 'sensitivity' of younger generations: turning the younger generations' practice of a feminism that refuses to betray trans women into the result of 'political correctness'. But these kinds of alliances are nothing new. In the past, anti-porn feminists Catherine McKinnon and Andrea Dworkin worked with right-wing think tanks bolstered by evangelical Christians to 'abolish' sex work. In the UK, TERF academics and public figures have opted for right-wing outlets to platform their views, and in the US, prominent feminist thinkers are now aligning themselves with the alt-right faces of free speech. TERFs teamed up with the Family Policy Alliance, a 'pro-family Christian group' to oppose Barack Obama's introduction of guidance on good policies and protections introduced at the federal level to help protect transgender students.

Short skirts, high heels

Another popular TERF argument is that, instead of challenging the gender binary, transitioning merely reaffirms it. To argue that trans women simply reaffirm a stereotypically 'feminine' model is to see all trans women as a homogenous group: feminine, heterosexual and wanting to transition. It ignores the fact that cis and trans women adopt stereotypical femininity for the same reason, blaming them for the gender scripts necessary for survival. In many cases, trans women may be actively encouraged by doctors and Gender Identity Clinics to adopt conventional femininity as a means of 'proving' that they are who they say they are. This proof would not be necessary in a different world. These kinds of requirements have far less to do with individuals and more to do with the way rigid ideas about gender are currently embedded in our social lives. The aim, at the very least, is to destroy that rigidity.

There are a diverse number of ways that trans women present. Many opt not to medically transition at all; many cannot even afford to consider it. Trans women are only asked to reject femininity in order to be granted 'citizenship' to womanhood because in the mind of cis gatekeepers, they are not really women. While it is crucial that we remain critical of how the sexist logics of capitalism are implicated in our self-image, we must also remember that rejecting femininity does not equal liberation. Women are not oppressed because of the existence of makeup or high heels or hair removal strips; these are merely by-products of a sexist society. This kind of thinking stems from a type of feminism that argues that women can escape sexist oppression by 'degendering' or refusing traditional femininity. While this approach opens our eyes to the fact that femininity is a construct that serves male dominance, opting for gender neutrality often means adopting a universalised masculinity. Baggy shirts and suits do not equal liberation either. Liberation cannot be ushered in by what we wear or how we speak or how we present ourselves. When we focus on the individual, we are asking the wrong question.

There is a dangerous liberal feminism that fetishises personal choice: Can you be a feminist and wear high heels? Can you be a feminist and shave your legs? But policing the way women present themselves distracts us from the more pressing issues at hand. Why are women the lowest paid workers? Why do women have the least access to the material resources necessary for survival? Are women free from violence? If not, then why not? The latter questions asks us to open our eyes and examine the way our society functions while the former are concerned with 'choice' as if choice exists in a vacuum. Our obsession with locating the singular universal cause of women's oppression stops us from engaging with the mechanisms of that oppression that manifest in daily life: the economic, the political, the social. This narrow scope for thinking about our own oppression has undoubtedly led many feminists to fall prey to the myth that trans women pose a threat to feminist advancements.

Transfeminist politics

Throughout history and in the present day, Transgender feminist theorists and activists have forged new ground. In her post-transexual manifesto, Sandy Stone questioned a society that requires trans people to medically transition in order to be accepted. 'Under the binary phallocratic founding myth by which Western bodies and subjects are authorised, only one body per gendered subject is "right". All other bodies are wrong.'[9] She urged instead, an embrace of unintelligibility and the pos-

---

9   Sandy Stone, 'The Empire Strikes Back: A Posttranssexual Manifesto,' *Camera Obscura: Feminism, Culture, and Media Studies* 10, (1992): 150–76.

sibility of chaos as a way to transform society. It is also trans theorists that have best articulated the specific kinds of violence faced by trans women. 'Transmisogyny' refers to the unique intersection of transphobia and misogyny. Coined in 2007 by Julia Serano in her book, *Whipping Girl*, it describes the intensification of misogyny that trans women experience because their femininity is viewed as fraudulent, inherently passive and existing solely in service of men and masculinity. Trans women are often punished for expressions of femininity. This ranges from fetishisation from men to physical violence to an outright denial of their womanhood.

TERFS create an antagonistic relationship between cis and trans women, presenting the latter as encroaching on the former. But this manufactured hostility elides feminist concerns. Feminists have long pointed out that women have an increased proximity to harm and that our lives are defined by it. Almost half of trans pupils in the UK have attempted suicide and Stonewall found that 41 per cent of trans respondents had been victims of a hate crime in the last 12 months.[10] If a feminist world is one without violence, establishing a hostile relationship between trans and cis women only serves as a distraction from identifying the root causes of the machinery of social organisation that put our lives at risk. Who wins in this scenario? How is violence eradicated? Whose lives are at stake while we separate 'real' women from 'fake' ones?

The limits of visibility

'The Trans Tipping Point,' dubbed by *Time* magazine in 2014 declared that a new wave of civil rights was emerging, ushered in

---

10   www.stonewall.org.uk/lgbt-britain-hate-crime-and-discrimination (last accessed 03/2019).

by the increased visibility of trans people. But when trans bodies become the subject of media speculation, the coverage tends to follow a specific narrative. Someone is born in the wrong body and they transition in order to fix this 'mistake'. They 'journey' from one binary gender to the other and when they 'arrive', all of their problems cease. The focus is on the trauma of the journey; again the logic of neo-liberalism boils trans experiences down to the physical body. The increased visibility of trans bodies afforded by the media rarely results in substantive changes to the quality of their everyday lives. It rarely results in increased safety or access to resources. An obsession with representation ensures we hear nothing of the reproductive injustices that mark transition; or waiting lists and gatekeeping from medical authorities, the sharing of medical information with the Home Office, or the fact that most Gender Identity Clinics are run by cisgender people with little practical knowledge of how to support those undergoing transition. Trans people are more likely than their cis counterparts to be poor, isolated from community, in precarious work and homeless. Focus on transition solves none of these problems. Cis obsession with trans bodies means that we hear nothing of the deaths of trans women in prisons across the country.

On their blog, Action for Trans Health, a grassroots organization fighting for democratic trans healthcare noted:

The first week of 2017 brought the tragic news that Jenny Swift had lost her life to suicide in HMP Doncaster, making a total of 4 known deaths of trans women prisoners in 14 months. Three of these – Jenny Swift, Joanne Latham and Vikki Thompson – were in men's prisons, while Nicola Cope died at Foston Hall women's prison in Derbyshire last November. Jenny Swift and Vikki Thompson both had their requests to be placed in women's prisons denied – Vikki had warned that she would kill herself if sent to a men's prison.[11]

As of yet, there is no government-sanctioned method of collecting data about the number of trans women murdered in the UK.

Imperfect endings

'Woman' is a strategic coalition, an umbrella under which we gather in order to make political demands. It might be mobilised in service of those who, given another option, would identify themselves in other ways. In a liberated future, it might not exist at all. It has no divine meaning absent of its function as a strategy; that does not mean we cannot feel, reckon with and grapple with our own private experiences of womanhood. For some, gender is an unshakeable truth and for others, it is always on the move. But a binary understanding of gender helps no one. When the urgency of gendered violence calls us to organise for solutions, we must look beyond our chromosomal make up to tell us who we are. The first step to crafting an expansive idea of gender is denaturalising it. While biology has served as a unifying focus point around which some feminist movements have advocated for rights and freedoms, we must accept that there are no easy answers. 'Woman' has never been a coherent group, it has always been a shifting category; 'woman' is frequently coded as cis, white and heterosexual. But it belongs to no one. Ignoring gender variance of all kinds for the sake of unity sacrifices our trans sisters and siblings. Recognising this means asking ourselves hard questions about the language we use when we organise, recognising the inclusions and exclusions

---

11   https://actionfortranshealth.org.uk/2017/01/ (last accessed 03/2019).

that are created by the mobilisation of womanhood and making peace with the fact that our current vocabularies can never fully capture the multiplicity we all contain.

Trans Exclusionary Radical Feminists have not only created a false dichotomy between cisgender and transgender women, they have managed to distract our attention away from the structures that determine the conditions of our lives and most importantly, ensure that all women are not free. We are all implicated in the violence against trans people when we allow their lives and the harm they face to be diminished by a media circus or when we enable TERFS to set the feminist narrative. As feminists, we have a duty to dismantle that circus and redirect the public imagination. Trans life is fundamental to our collective liberation.

Chapter 5

The saviour complex: Muslim women and gendered Islamophobia

Could we not leave veils and vocations of saving others behind
and instead train our sights on ways to make the world a more
just place? – Lila Abu-Lughod

I want us to rise up because passivity and heedless cooper-
ation only earn us betrayal and death. Inshallah, we will
survive this – but we need to be able to count on one another.
– Muna Mire

Muslim women rarely qualify as individuals whose bodies
deserve to be protected, cared for or centred in feminist debates.
The Muslim woman is spoken for, not spoken to; imposed upon,
invaded, dissected; rarely treated as an autonomous human
being whose freedom deserves to be understood on their own
terms. When Muslim women are spoken of in the media, they
are empty caricatures or victims suffering under the patriarchal
control of their father and brothers. They are in constant need
of saving: from themselves, from each other, from 'backward
nations', but never from contemporary forms of governance that
increasingly place their lives at risk. Muslim women know best

67

how to speak about their own lives and have been doing so for centuries, exposing how the convergence of patriarchal states, interpersonal violence, racialisation and violent misogyny shape their navigation of the world.

The rhetoric of 'British Values' frames our understandings of social life in the UK. The way we talk about Britishness and belonging is bound up with race and gender, as markers of who should be included under the nation's protection and who should not. We've been told of the so-called 'British Values' we should be proud of – democracy, liberty, the rule of law, mutual respect, tolerance. Politicians use this phrase to dictate the 'correct' way to be a citizen, justifying violence against those who they deem transgressive as a way to protect these 'values' at all costs. The state argues that it endeavours to protect women from the violent extremists that seek to threaten 'our' way of life. Because of its uncritical reliance on the state, mainstream feminism mimics this language. But what if, as feminists, we stepped beyond the nation? We know that Islamophobia continuously props up Muslim men as enemies of the state, so Muslim women inevitably become their accomplices in the public imagination. This leaves no room to understand the complex and multilayered nature of Muslim women's lives in Britain.

Islamophobia is the social and political assumption that Muslims are predisposed to violence. It manifests itself in a number of different ways: exposure to violence and premature death, workplace discrimination, harassment, surveillance, retraction of citizenship, 'secular' restrictions on religious clothing, racist media coverage, hyper-visibility. It is the public rejoicing at 19-year-old Shamima Begum being stripped of her citizenship after being groomed online by members of ISIS. It is the predictable cycles of public mourning in which Muslims are asked to denounce terror as if they were collectively responsible.

It is the way that Islam is scapegoated as the singular cause of 'global terror' and the way that the state's increasingly authoritarian responses are 'justified' under the guise of protection of its citizens. Islamophobia is a cultural environment that allowed the sitting UK Prime Minister, Boris Johnson, to compare women who wear the niqab to 'letterboxes' in a national newspaper with no repercussions. The image of the black and brown terrorist has become the defining feature of media coverage in the last decade. When this image is used to create a false moral panic about the impending danger of 'terrorism' from those who despise 'the West' and all that it stands for, Muslim women face the consequences. Their bodies become the playground for racist misogyny. Since 2015, there has been a sharp rise in physical and verbal attacks on Muslims in public spaces. The Islamic Human Rights Commission conducted a survey and found a 40 per cent rise in the number of respondents who said they had witnessed abuse or discrimination directed at Muslims between 2010 and 2015.[1]

In order to counter Islamophobia as feminists, it is important to understand the way that government surveillance of Muslim life has intensified since the September 11 attacks in 2001, and the role that gender played in justifying the subsequent war in Afghanistan and invasion of Iraq. It is crucial to remember that 9/11 did not invent the surveillance of Muslims. The history of Empire is littered with examples of attempts to civilise, control and expel Muslims who were viewed as a threat to Western Christianity. Black Muslims have always felt the full force of the state; to be black is already to be considered a threat, to move through the world knowing that your body elicits a broad range of reactions: fear, disgust, anger, annoyance. The overlap of state

---

1   www.theguardian.com/world/2015/nov/11/majority-of-british-muslims-have-witnessed-islamophobia-study (last accessed 03/2019).

racism, racism in Muslim communities and the erasure of black-ness in the history of Islam means that black Muslim women especially, have become a figment of our imaginations. If 9/11 marks the point of the intensification of the counter terrorism regime, black Muslim women living in and outside of the West have always known that the conditions they are subjected to challenge the freedom that feminism promises us. Muna Mire writes 'The hypervisibility of Blackness makes one's identity as a Muslim impossible precisely because Blackness precludes Muslimness in the cultural imaginary. So to occupy both subject positions is to experience the downward thrust of cognitive dissonance.'[2]

White saviours

On the 14 September 2010, French parliament banned the wearing of the niqab in public spaces. Zaynab Hussein sus-tained serious injuries after being hit and run over by a car in Leicester driven by a man who claimed he 'wanted revenge' for terrorist attacks in London in September 2017. In New York, Soha Salama was kicked down the stairs and called a terrorist while commuting to work. She was rushed to hospital with leg injuries. In 2018, a 19-year-old Muslim woman was attacked in a hospital waiting room in Dearborn, Michigan. In November 2018, A British man was put on trial for sending hundreds of racist letters to addresses across the country encouraging others to 'punish' Muslims and promising a donation of £100 for each killing. The very real consequences of Islamophobia are expe-rienced in daily acts of violence towards Muslim women. In a society where there are few repercussions for violence against

2 https://thenewinquiry.com/towards-a-black-muslim-ontology-of-resistance (last accessed 03/2019).

women, Muslim women are easy targets because their pain is invisible to so-called systems of justice and to a liberal feminism whose definition of womanhood is premised on their exclusion.

In the public eye, Muslim women's bodies have always been a site of contestation. 'Impassioned' arguments about freedom, agency and belonging are mapped onto their skin by the state and by mainstream feminists. 'The veil' has taken centre stage in recent decades. This debate has been powerful in shaping the way we view and think about the existence of Muslim women. The 'oppressed' versus 'liberated' binary has distorted perceptions of Muslim women, making it near impossible for them to *be* anything else in the public imagination. If feminism means freedom, it means the right to self-determination and the right to be multi-dimensional, disorganised and even incoherent. The current understanding of Muslim women's bodies as either belonging to the state or to their family is incompatible with a radical feminist vision of freedom. 'The veil' has justified wars, it has changed laws and it has become one of the most contentious symbols in the modern world. A feminist politics that strives to create dignified lives for all recognises how public debates about the veil turn visibly Muslim women into targets for gendered violence. There is much at stake when colonial, one-dimensional ideas about religion become weaponised in the name of 'feminism'. White feminists have mobilised the image of the oppressed Muslim woman to justify a global 'war on terror' turning Muslim women's bodies into the site through which the nation conducts its business. This obscures the very urgent problems that feminists should be attentive to: Muslim women are the most economically disenfranchised group in the country.

According to the Department of Work and Pensions, 58 per cent of all Muslim women were economically inactive in 2015. They are three times as likely to be unemployed than their non-Muslim

ist or extremist activity. It is split into four streams, Prevent, Pursue, Protect and Prepare. The Prevent strand of this strategy is intended to help 'identify' the early signs of radicalisation. One of the key ways this is achieved is by monitoring the consumption and activities of those deemed 'most at risk' in order to screen for 'anti-Western' sentiments. The government has mandated all public institutions to comply with the Prevent Duty. The state has given schools, universities, the NHS and other public institutions keys to our civic lives to determine what they deem 'extremist' behaviour and use any means necessary to prevent it. In a world where the constructed figure of the extremist is coded as Muslim, this kind of legislation encroaches on the privacy and rights of Muslims, cordoning off their lives for scrutiny and inspection.

Muslim women are viewed as complicit in the 'radicalisation' process. They are perceived as the gatekeepers of their communities and reproducers of cultural values. In the eyes of the state, they give birth to the next generation and influence the conversations that happen in their homes and the ideas that their children engage with. When Conservative Prime Minister David Cameron announced a government roll out of English classes in 2016 especially for Muslim women in an effort to 'curb' radicalisation, he not only revealed that the government viewed extremism as a specifically 'Muslim' problem but that Muslim women could be utilised by the government to exert their agenda.

Because she does not belong to herself and she does not exist outside of her role as child-rearer, spouse, mother, the Muslim woman is the perfect symbol for anti-radicalisation measures. Not only is this deeply sexist, it leaves no room to understand how Muslim women exist outside of the family. It leaves no room to view them as human beings with conflicting sets of desires, thoughts and needs. When women's lives are considered only in relation to what they can do for others, they are not viewed as worth protecting in their own right. This thinking should ring alarm bells in the minds of critical feminists and yet has been actively encouraged by mainstream feminism. In 2015, Grace Dent gleefully argued that young women groomed by ISIS 'shouldn't be allowed back into the country ever'[5] and in 2018, Polly Toynbee argued that the niqab was a symbol of religious fundamentalism.[6] In our fight for agency, we must not fall into the trap of viewing Muslim women simply as vehicles for extremism. A staunchly secular way of thinking about our lives and bodies limits Muslim women's ability to understand themselves and our ability to provide meaningful solidarity when they become the targets of far-right extremism.

In 2003, The British government entered into an alliance with the Bush White House to invade Afghanistan with the expressed desire to 'liberate' women from patriarchal 'barbarians'. Laura Bush's infamous radio address stated 'Life under the Taliban is so hard and repressive, even small displays of joy are outlawed – children aren't allowed to fly kites; their mothers face beatings for laughing out loud. Women cannot work outside the home, or even leave their homes by themselves.' Every battle against 'Islamic extremism' waged by governments rests on a simplistic idea of the Muslim woman as submissive, passive bearers of violence. As argued by Lila Abu-Lughod, perhaps Muslim women do not need saving, perhaps they require a feminist solidarity that recognises their existence, activism and knowledge;

---

5   www.independent.co.uk/voices/comment/if-teenage-girls-want-to-join-isis-in-the-face-of-all-its-atrocities-then-they-should-leave-and-10065516.html (last accessed 03/2019).

6   www.theguardian.com/commentisfree/2018/aug/14/boris-johnson-burqa-dehumanise-muslim-women (last accessed 03/2019).

one that mobilises in order to defend them against an increasingly hostile world.

'Terror'

In an age of government bans on Muslims travelling between countries, the stripping of citizenship and the fortification of borders, public conversations about Muslim people legitimises white supremacist terrorist violence against them. The 2019 Christchurch attack in New Zealand, in which a white supremacist and member of the 'alt-right' killed 51 people in a mosque, calls for sober reflection. More than a meditation on the brutality of the act itself, this massacre reminds us of the urgency of the situation we find ourselves in. Feminism can no longer remain a rhetorical tool; it must have teeth. It must fight back by providing us with a way of analysing global violence and laying the foundations to combat it. It is important for us to draw the links between media coverage, narratives about terrorism and the rise of the white supremacist, fascist right who act in order to vindicate their ideas about Muslim people as threats to social order, democracy and 'freedom'. White masculinity is mobilised in these specific acts of racist violence: this is no coincidence.

White men are radicalised online as a direct result of the political narratives about Islam encouraged by the state; Anders Breivik, responsible for the death of 77 people in Norway in 2011 wrote a 1,500 page dossier in which he cited feminism and Islam as the causes of 'Europe's cultural suicide'. Thomas Mair, an avowed white nationalist, former member of the BNP and other far-right groups, who consistently targeted Muslims, murdered MP Jo Cox in 2016. Darren Osborne murdered Makram Ali and wounded several others when he drove a van into passersby near Finsbury Park Mosque in 2018 with the intention of killing Muslims. It is not enough to look at troubling acts of white supremacist violence through the lens of masculinity or to simply name them 'terrorist'. White supremacists do not only commit acts of terror because masculinity is bound up with violence and domination. Many members of the far right have publicly referred to themselves as engaged in a battle against Muslims or against extremism, signalling the collusion of racism and violent misogyny. The white supremacist desire for power expresses itself through masculine violence and so the fight for feminists is two-fold. Rather than dismiss these murders as unavoidable, we must look at how white supremacy and masculinity converge, ask why both seem to sit so comfortably together and develop strategies to dismantle both.

Inherent to the rise of fascism across Europe is the war being waged in the name of 'white working class girls'. Young girls have become the bargaining chips that fascists use to recruit members. Stephen Yaxley Lennon more commonly known as Tommy Robinson is an Islamophobic 'far-right' talking head who has been a key figure in the creation of a public outcry about 'Asian Grooming Gangs.' Following reporting on child sexual exploitation rings, his racialised public comments have characterised Muslim men as uniquely paedophilic in order to make the case that the far-right are the only group coming to the defence of the most vulnerable members of the 'white working class'. Here we see the mobilisation of white girlhood as vulnerability, completely ignoring how the police and social authorities routinely fail white working class girls who are subject to child sexual exploitation. This framing also ignores Muslim victims of child sexual exploitation in order to present the far right as heroic saviours who seek to 'protect women and girls' when political correctness places them in danger. These tactics are not new: women's bodies have always been co-opted to legitimise harm and exclusion against those deemed a threat.

Groups like the Feminist Anti-Fascist Assembly have taken a bold stance against the symbolic use of women and girls by fascists. In 2018, they led a militant bloc at the front of a counter-protest demonstration against the far-right Democratic Football Lads Alliance.[7] As feminists, we must understand the damage that cementing these ideas does and boldly proclaim that white nationalists have never, and could never speak on our behalf because they do not care about us. White nationalists care about women and children insofar as they can be used to push their racist, sexist agenda. Liberal feminism does not have an answer to this far-right co-optation because it has yet to properly contend with race, the violence of the state border or fascism. Building a more critical feminism involves extending feminist protection to all. Any feminism that pathologises religion locks out the opportunity to reckon with the distinct brutality that Muslim women are subjected to. When Muslim women are dying at such alarming rates across the world, this is a fatal error.

Subversion

Muslim feminists across the diaspora have been at the forefront of the political imagining of liberated futures. They have demonstrated that the lives of Muslim women are not defined by misery by using art and activism to subvert the various gazes placed on them. It is a feminist act to speak back, enact and embed resistance into our daily lives.

---

7 www.redpepper.org.uk/anti-fascism-is-feminist-issue (last accessed 03/2019).

It's easy for the work I do to become just an attempt to satiate a white consumptive gaze . . . it's a twofold thing, there is gaze upon you that is very crushing, but also a gaze that is consumptive. There is a simultaneous derision and demand for Muslim women. The way that I try to subvert that is by putting a lot of onus on the audience . . . I never divulge my trauma for a sake of an audience, I'm constantly trying to flip the mirror back to say, no actually, this is about you. It's very easy as a visibly Muslim woman in the public gaze to want to be liked, it is very appealing to be granted humanity . . . but I try to think, can I challenge this audience? Can I unsettle them, can I get them to admit to themselves that they didn't see me as human?

As a feminist poet, activist and educator, Suhaiymah Manzoor Khan tells me that her work attempts to force the audience to examine their own complicity in the violence Muslim women experience and create a space where the normalisation of that violence is unsettled. Her artistic practice is combative, expanding what is possible for Muslim women in the public eye. She is not seeking approval or validation from the mainstream; her understanding of Islamophobia is rooted in histories of colonialism and racism. She understands that instances of Islamophobia do not happen in isolation but are a direct consequence of a long-established colonial order predicated on dehumanisation:

During the French occupation of Algeria, soldiers would have public unveilings of Muslim women . . . it was a public showing meant to demonstrate the superiority of French culture. Nobody cared about the lives of those women, their stories or histories. They were just symbols . . . I see this as directly linked to the treatment of Shamima Begum, we don't care about her background, her context, who is she, her circumstances, it just becomes about the image of the Jihadi Bride.

For her, this work is feminist work because:

If we understand feminism as liberation from gendered oppression, Islamophobia has a very significant impact on the way that people experience gender and the way that they are gendered. The construction of the Muslim woman itself is a very insidious thing, the reason we are made out to be the way that we are is to justify particular kinds of violence.

In activist spaces, world building is a key part of the organising process. You imagine the world you wish to see and then work towards it. When Muslim women think about the future, what do they think about? Feminist activist and former NUS Women's Officer Hareem Ghani tells me her vision:

A world without borders . . . the reason I say that is because I'm against this idea of statehood or nationhood. So much of what Muslim women are experiencing, whether that's access to reproductive healthcare, whether that's being used as a vehicle for counter-terrorism measures to spy on their communities . . . those issues wouldn't exist in a world without borders. The whole reason this image is painted, of Muslim women being oppressed and Muslim men being patriarchal and oppressive is so that the state can crack down on them and justify the closing of borders. It's a way to outsource blame, to say problems with rape culture or domestic violence do not belong to us, they come from an alien culture imported into the UK . . . Without this idea of nation, there isn't a sense of 'British Values' to demarcate who belongs and who doesn't.

While a world without borders may seem far-fetched to some, borders themselves inform the treatment of Muslim women across the world. In 2015 and 2016, the Missing Migrants project estimated that 5,000 people lost their lives attempting to seek asylum across borders. An estimated 746 people have lost their lives in 2019 alone. A feminist politics that is about creating a world free from harm must make connections between the lives of British-born Muslims and the Muslims who die in transit, between nations.

A core part of the Muslim feminist project is calling attention to the gaps in feminist organising in the UK. For Muslim feminist activists, building networks and coalitions across feminist groups is part of the process of shifting feminist concern away from the image of the Muslim woman towards the reality of her material conditions. Hareem understands the centrality of this process:

A big thing that gets left out of discussions about Muslim women is the 'Chill Factor'. A lot of Muslim women avoid going into public spaces and running for public positions because of the inevitable harassment they will receive. We need to link these findings to feminist organising in the UK. We need to begin to make those connections. For example, why does Reclaim The Night, an annual march that purports to focus on harassment, and the violence that women face in public spaces, not attend to the specific way this manifests in the lives of Muslim women, who are having their hijabs and nijabs ripped off in the street?

White saviour complexes conceal the very real relationship between Islamophobia, capitalism, race and colonial history. By recognising that conditions for Muslims in Britain worsen day by day, we can begin to formulate a strategic response to the way that the state and global powers attempt to regulate and diminish Muslim life. This starts by reconsidering everything we *think* we know about Muslim women.

Chapter 6

Art for art's sake

Let me tell you:
We can't individually 'win' in this world
& simultaneously create another
Together. – Wendy Trevino

We must also broaden our conception of what it means to be creative. At best, one of the most creative activities is being involved in a struggle with other people, breaking out of our isolation, seeing our relations with others change, discovering new dimensions in our lives. – Silvia Federeci

I would rather write nothing at all than propagandise for the world as is. – Anne Boyer

In 1985, Mona Hatoum walks the streets of Brixton barefoot with doc martens wrapped around her ankles. She places one foot in front of the other decisively for an hour. Her performance is captured and edited into a six-minute colour video. *Roadworks* is born. As a member of the Brixton Art Collective, her piece makes a powerful intervention in public space – a space defined by police brutality, the ritual of stop and search and the infrastructure of impoverishment imposed on communities from above. Hatoum wished to bring her art into public view, to have live interactions with the people who walked the streets beside her. Her performance piece gets beyond the limits of the gallery space, takes art outside, through the puddles that litter the streets. The boots, tightly wrapped around her ankles, signify mechanisms of state control. The same boots were worn by violently racist skinheads and the police: Hatoum invites the audience to make the connection.

cecile emeke's subject is the black flaneur in soft focus. Her mini-documentary series follows members of the African diaspora. One subject speaks directly to the camera about the afterlife of slavery and colonialism in France. The camera lingers and follows, being led by the speaker – it permits us access to a set of ideas, discourses and emotions. Critique is central to emeke's strolling series. It was born out of a desire to document the conversations she had been a part of for years. The flaneur walks forward, unafraid.

Barby Asante's *Declarations of Independence* is being realised as a series of project episodes. It is in keeping with her tradition of mapping stories, utilising the archive through dialogue: a way of speaking in all directions. It has included public installation of a forum at the BALTIC bringing womxn of colour together to 'explore the social, cultural and political agency of women of colour, as they navigate historic legacies of colonialism, independence, migration and the contemporary global socio-political climate.'

* * *

Visual art, painting, sculpture, photography and literature provide a space for us to test our limits. They are mediums for meditation and reflection. Art moves us because it provokes feelings and calls for a response. Whether that response is repulsion, fear, joy, appreciation, or boredom – art calls for a witness. Perhaps it is this same desire to witness that is the driving force behind the work of feminist activists. As feminists, we are moved by injustice in the world, we work because what is happening around us demands a response. Our responses are varied and aren't limited to the sphere of 'the political.' We do a disservice to the power of art and artistic creation when we assume that it is less important than political intervention, likewise we do ourselves a disservice when we assume that art alone can liberate us.

What happens when we consume a piece of art? We might feel emotional, nostalgic, inspired – a space is opened up where feeling those things isn't silly or self-indulgent but instinctive. The conditions of our lives: the need to work, the expectation of domestic, manual and emotional labour, mean that there is rarely time or space for artistic reflection. But art can abstract us from the demands placed on our bodies at any given time. It can remind us that we do not only exist in relation to our gendered responsibilities: we are not only someone's mother or sister, or carer – we are individuals brimming with sophisticated ideas. Creativity is at the heart of any new world we seek to build. Without the demands placed on our body by capital, by gender and by race – we could be freed up to read, write and to create. Alongside political freedom comes an escape from the social conditioning that deadens our creativity. Every time we engage our creative faculties, we are going against a logic that places work and the nuclear family at the centre of our existence. Art is threatening because when produced under the right conditions, it cannot be controlled. But gatekeepers and cultural institutions have written women, especially black women, outside of the history of artistic creation and freedom.

84

ART FOR ART'S SAKE

The idea of *Art for Art's Sake* suggests that art has the ability to escape the conditions of its creation, the contexts and motivations it arises from. In many ways, this is a core part of the feminist project; escaping the naming of your body, your personhood, disrupting the inevitability of violence. We are always trying to escape the conditions of our lives and there is no doubt that artistic practice helps us do this. But when we imply that the sole purpose of art is helping rediscover a shared 'humanity' or a way of feeling that is not dependent on time, location and all of the other markers that organise our lives, we blunt the knife that might help us tear these markers down. Art is best utilised as a weapon, a writing back, as evidence that we were here. Apolitical approaches, or approaches that seek to deaden the resistant potential of artistic practice are merely another mechanism through which the status quo is reproduced.

'Can we separate the art from the artist?' is a tired debate often rehashed when feminists note the violent origins of otherwise beautiful creations. While it is possible to have a positive experience of art produced by an individual who has perpetrated harm, perhaps it is more important to realise that art alone cannot repair harm. If we want art that reflects the true complexity of our lives and the range of human emotion, then we must eradicate the harmful conditions in which we live. As much as artists may run away from the political underpinnings of their work, it haunts them. Art is powerful, but it is not powerful enough to undo centuries of colonial domination or climate catastrophe. It is only as effective as we allow it to be. We give art its agency and healing ability: we enable it to speak to the painful, shameful and most delicate aspects of our lives. That is a responsibility, one that we all have a role in upholding. Although the experience of witnessing art may feel context-less and universal, the idea that it can cross difference and get to the

in rethinking the purpose of art, it is helpful to think about the long tradition of feminists using all kinds of creative mediums to make something out of their activist work. Art is a tool for feminist propaganda; it can help us craft a future that does not yet exist. As feminists, remaining attentive to the artistic and cultural conversations that dominate public life is as significant as remaining attentive to the political narratives that are circulating; both inform one another. That space that art opens up reminds us that despite the violence we are subjected to, there are still parts of our minds that cannot be controlled.

Who gets to make art?

A series of portraits of a black woman, plain clothing, a head wrap. The images intend to explore spirituality and rituals of her Gambian heritage. At points her face is obscured, her hands covering her eyes. The photographs point to a lineage. They are a reworking of pre-colonial subjectivity. The edges are faded, the colouring mimicking that of nineteenth century portraiture. An attempt to meet history. A way of glancing backwards to the women whose stories we do not know, a nod to ancestors, a claiming of place. A commentary on the past, present and future.

The Venice Biennale is an arts organisation based in Venice, which is home to the Art Biennale, a contemporary visual art exhibition that is hosted biannually. The prestige of the exhibition has launched the careers of many artists, their work subsequently receiving critical acclaim. In early 2017, in the diaspora Pavilion, Khadija's Saye's series of photographs entitled *Dwelling: In this space we breathe* were displayed. A few months later in June, Saye died in the Grenfell tower fire. She was only 24 years of age. The divide between politics and art is not real. It is politics that dictates who creates art, how it is consumed and sold, the conditions in which it is created, the subjectivities that dominate it. Poor women do not get to make art: the fact that Saye's work could be displayed in one of the most prestigious arenas in the world, while government neglect ensured that she would meet death in a circumstance that could so easily have been avoided calls us to wake up to the cruelty of inequity. As feminists, if we wish to see a world of art and creativity, then we must remove the barriers to that creativity and the systems that kill artists. We must dismantle the systems of poverty, racism, incarceration, impoverishment that leave so many women unable to fulfil their creative potential. Art requires will. But it also requires, as writer Virginia Woolf recognises, a room of one's own. A set of social and financial circumstances that enable creativity to take place. The question of who gets to make art is inseparable from questions of liberation and freedom.

In the UK, working class women artists are not only under-represented, but actively excluded from the opportunities, internships and mentoring schemes that might equip them with the skills and resources to develop their artistry. Black women artists suffer under the burden of representation set by liberal arts organisations that refuse to consider their work beyond narrowly conceived ideas of 'identity' or as markers of cultural diversity.[2] But feminist art and the creative process belong to all of us. The task is not to recover creativity from the gatekeepers but to expand the scope of what counts as artistic creation. Navigating the world with a feminist consciousness requires creativity, it requires innovative responses to being consumed, surveilled, violated, denigrated, mocked and humiliated. But we rarely call ourselves artists: we rarely call resistance, art.

---

2   www.theguardian.com/culture/2019/feb/12/english-arts-bodies-slow-to-become-more-diverse-report-shows (last accessed 03/2019).

There is that Toni Cade Bambara quote, 'The role of the artist is to make the revolution irresistible . . . It's really important to think about the liberatory potential of your work, that doesn't mean it has to be didactic. It can be achieved by who you choose to humanise, who you choose to centre, the questions that you ask. Artists play a big role in asking questions and imagining freedom dreams beyond limitations . . . the artist's role is to think beyond their time.

Momtaza Mehri, essayist, researcher and former Poet Laureate for young people, tells me. By making the revolution irresistible, the artist breathes life into movements and provides an added dimension that political discourses can sometimes fail to capture. An alliance between art and politics enables us to not only expand the scope of creativity: it gives more women the license to understand the artistic as well as political circumstances of their lives. In her own work, Mehri is interested in the generative potential of dissent:

I'm interested in artistic beef. I love when it opens up room for discussion and it's interesting and generative. I love the debates the black art movement had about Black nationalism versus third worldism vs black internationalism . . . I love that they had arguments about which journals to submit to, The New York Times versus Underground black arts journals.

The tension created by political literary and artistic disagreements highlights how important critique is to movements for liberation. In the UK, young publications like *The White Pube*, run by Gabrielle de la Puente and Zarina Muhammad are democratising art criticism by removing it from the grips of institutions and placing it back into the hands of young feminist

thinkers attentive to race, gender, class and the activist potential of the art we consume. Their online art criticism follows
the tradition of young women choosing non-traditional forms
of media to counter elitist gatekeeping. *The White Pube* belongs
to a history of radical print and online cultures commandeered
by young women who used art as a means of self-actualisation.
The pamphlet has a coveted place in feminist history, as does
the radical printing press. The emergence of zines during punk
movements in 90s London and New York allowed complete edi-
torial freedom and a place to make art without any rules. This
legacy is continued in British publications like *OOMK* (One of
My Kind) and *The Khidr Collective*, who choose to remain inde-
pendent, flexible and give young artists a place to showcase
work outside of institutional approval.

Insurrectionary artistic practice is a necessary call to action
for feminists. But women's concerns have never been identical
and so feminist artistic practice does not have a linear history,
much like the feminist movement. Much of 'second wave'
American visual art made by white women was centred on the
body, sex and rebelling against domestic space because these
were the priorities of the middle class feminist movement at the
time. Black women artists have always had different priorities,
no matter what generation they belong to. African American
artists like Carrie Mae Weems, Lorna Simpson and Betye Saar
and Black British artists Lubiana Himid, Claudette Johnson and
Maud Salter focused on questions of black women's subjectivity
and interiority, social meanings of blackness and the afterlife of
slavery. Mehri says,

> We have to find a way to analyse things in a way that learns
> from the past, which is why intergenerational dialogue
> between feminists is so important. There's a cultural memory

that gets lost every time you surround yourself only with people who are your age.

A glance back into history of popular and legitimised art demonstrates how hierarchies that exist in everyday life are reproduced. It forces us to consider whose art is held up as evidence of the movement and whose work is forgotten. Perhaps most pertinently, does the most admired feminist art threaten social and political order? If the purpose of art in a feminist context is to raise consciousness, then perhaps the most important art movements are those locked away in the archive, movements that took place outside the world of mainstream recognition.

For Mehri, the influence of feminism on her work is structural, rather than a topic of concern, it is intrinsic to her understanding of the world:

A feminist framework, if it does the work of clarifying and not obscuring, has done its job. Clarifying the machinery of our lives as woman with all our identifying markers, clarifying the role we play in dismantling the machinery of exploitation.

Perhaps the artist can say and do things that the political activist cannot, but the prestigious world of visual art and literature can often remove us from the reality of the life-saving work happening on the ground in the communities we inhabit. A well-known literary journal or gallery may in some ways be a sacred space but it can also serve as a vehicle for depoliticisation. Art must be democratic to be useful, when I ask Momtaza about the future, she tells me:

I think about the order and episteme we live under right now, it's so totalising that it is hard to think about what is beyond it . . . What is poetry outside of capitalism? I can't tell you because I've never experienced that. But I do know that more people will be able to be poets. I do know that the form might change and be more accessible to people.

A democratic vision of art is one where creativity belongs to the most exploited, the women who do not immediately spring to mind when we hear the word 'artist.'

The archive

Soweto blues – they are killing all the children/Soweto blues – without any publicity/Soweto blues – oh, they are finishing the nation/Soweto blues – while calling it black on black.

When Miriam Makeba lent her voice to Hugh Masekela's protest song about the brutal police response to the Soweto Uprising in 1976, it became a rallying cry for an entire generation. This example from the archive demonstrates how powerful a feminist use of art can be. Women's voices and bodies often become symbols of resistance but their vital contributions to political movements are lost. Makeba used her voice to expose the violence of the apartheid regime. Feminists can seize control of the public imagination and command a global conversation using a variety of forms. This is only one example of how artistic resistances can reach others across contexts. It reminds us that contemporary feminism has a long legacy to draw from.

Our practical struggle become[s] what it must be: the realisation of our basic principles in the process of social life and the embodiment of our general principles in practical every day action. And only under these conditions do we fight in the sole permissible way for what is at any time 'possible'. – Rosa Luxemburg

In *Art of the Possible: Towards an Antifascist Feminist Front*, Artist Sanja Ivekovic invited writer Angela Dimitrakaki and theorist Antonia Majaca to create an audio intervention to accompany her installations *Monument to Revolution* (2017) in Athens, Greece. The piece responds to the monument created by Ludwig Mies der Rohe's in honour of revolutionaries Rosa Luxemburg and Karl Leibknet in Berlin, which was destroyed by the Nazis in the 1930s. The two hour long clip is a compilation of reflections, words and sounds from over 30 contributors engaged in the fight against fascism across the world including Kurdistan, Mexico, France, Indonesia and Singapore. It is an attempt to document a struggle as it happens, to build an internationalist feminist framework able to respond to fascist violence, forge bonds of solidarity, recognise the specificity of the moment we are currently in and the history that created it.

The audio clip is an example of the ways feminist activists and artists have collaborated to make meaningful public interventions that refuse to lose sight of the urgency of the current moment. It is also an attempt to rewrite the history of revolution, to acknowledge that women have been responsible for creating and sustaining movements. As well as exposing the most prominent features of fascist regimes, the clip explores possibility and futurity and affirms the impact of recognising feminist goals as something that are entirely realisable. It is a mini-manifesto, a consciousness-raising tool and rousing reminder that we are alive now, in this political moment and it is our responsibility to respond. 'To speak as if it were possible to have a voice in common, to speak as if it were possible that that voice in common could gain momentum,' one voice in the recording says.

Feminist art can call us to attention: making us want to stand up and be counted. That indescribable feeling that marks dissent: protest, the speaking up, coming out and refusing to be a good woman, a good girl, a good capitalist subject. When feminist art is able to bridge the gap between grassroots movements and the theory that commands them, a stronger coalitional politics emerges. Art alone cannot beat the rise of fascism but it is one of the many tools that we can use to destabilise it.

Art for Art's Sake cannot exist while any of us are unfree. Feminists have long rejected the idea because they know that every artistic creation has a social and political meaning. They have instead used art for the sake of a political vision, art for the sake of our lives and our happiness. Assata Shakur's famous refrain 'It is our duty to fight for our freedom/it is our duty to win/we must love and support one another/we have nothing to lose but our chains,' repositions the fight against injustice as a task we are obliged to partake in. Feminist art is moralising and instructive because this is necessary ammunition when our lives are on the line. It helps us clarify our position and make sense of what it is we are imagining. When we engage in political work, we do so for every artist that cannot become an artist because they are black, poor, uneducated, disabled, trans, because structural barriers mean that their lives are already mapped out for them. We use art to fight political battles in order to create the conditions for unbridled creativity. So that we might all be able to live artistic lives: lives of freedom.

Chapter 7

Complicating consent: How to support sex workers

The only way to eliminate prostitution is to eliminate this society which creates the need. – Young Lord's Party Position on Women, 1970

People get really hung up on the question, 'Well, would you want your daughter doing it?' That's the wrong question. Instead, imagine she is doing it. How safe is she at work tonight? Why isn't she safer? – Juno Mac

We chant it on the streets, we hear it in workshops, we print it on tote bags, stickers, t-shirts. *Whatever we wear, wherever we go, yes means yes and no means no.* This phrase has come to define a generation's understanding of sex. It's a necessary attempt to reclaim our agency and autonomy. It is a rallying cry that affirms that women are not responsible for the violence that is inflicted on them and that if only men would pay attention, listen for a sign, stay attentive to body language, it could be avoided. It is an angry chant; it gives us a place to put our rage. And why shouldn't we be angry? In a world where one in three women will experience sexual violence in her lifetime,[1] why should we behave as if this is a normal state of affairs? For women, violation becomes an expected part of growing up, an initiation into womanhood; a rite of passage.

#MeToo has propelled conversations about sexual violence into the mainstream. Liberal feminism argues that learning about consent is the antidote to men's violent expressions of masculinity. If we sit men down, train them rigorously, disrupt disturbing patterns of behaviour, then we stand a chance. But in the rush to push knowledge about consent into the public eye, liberal feminists have neglected how power underpins all of our sexual relations. Their focus on the simplicity of sexual encounters paints an incomplete picture of the different *kinds* of sex that take place in society. Their rhetoric has placed sex workers at the centre of an ideological battle about what kinds of sexual encounters are 'acceptable'.

The happy face of consent

In order to sell consent, liberal feminists adopted language that would appeal to the masses. They told us that consent was easy; a verbal confirmation, always enthusiastic, always sober. The consequences of this thinking trickled into countless institutions. In 2015, The Thames Valley Police released a video analogising consent to making someone a cup of tea in an attempt to underline how *simple* it is. If you want to make someone a cup of tea and they refuse – don't force them to drink it. This video and many others like this were widely shared on social media. But this analogy not only downplays the severity of sexual violence; it assumes that rape only occurs because of misread signals.

---

1 www.who.int/news-room/fact-sheets/detail/violence-against-women (last accessed 04/2019).

Consent is not like tea. Consent allows us to express an agency that makes us feel like we exist. It is fundamental. To compare it to a process as mundane as making tea not only makes a mockery of the experiences of survivors, it betrays a misunderstanding of how gendered power relations work. Rapists know that rape is wrong and still commit it because of a sense of entitlement to someone else's bodily autonomy. This is not something that can be fixed by merely asking rapists not to rape; women have been making this plea for centuries to no avail.

This 'happy face' of consent coincided with a rise in sex-positive feminism, which placed pleasure at the core of under-standing sexual relations. Sex positivity views sex as an inherently good, liberating and ultimately, an exciting practice for women. It demands that as women we reclaim pleasure by knowing our bodies and demanding that our needs and wants are met in the bedroom. Sex-positive feminism dictates that if it *feels* good, then it is good. Under this rubric, some sex positive feminists argue that sex work is an empowering personal choice made by individuals who like it. Consent is framed as an enhancement of pleasure rather than a requirement for an individual to express agency. 'Consent is sexy!' began to appear on fresher's leaflets and in workshops as a way to convince men that sex is a shared experienced. But this approach left no space for ambivalence, no space for sex as a mundane activity, no space for sex as transactional, which it can often be. Sex positivity eroded the relationship between sex and power. While a lot of the ideas advocated by sex positivity might be beneficial on an individual level, its major failure was oversimplifying the notion of consent by portraying it as something that occurs exclusively in the domain of sex and romance and not as the basis of every decision we make in our society.

Developing a more robust understanding of consent requires us to reconsider it. We have to ask, is consent always enthusiastic?

If we engage in sex unenthusiastically, have we still consented? What if you're tired or suffering from a chronic illness? What if you know that in exchange for sex, you'll be able to feed your kids for the next three days? What does consent mean then? Sex is complicated and it is made more complicated by the inter-web of power relations that define the ways we relate to one another. At a structural level, sexual violence is a deliberate occurrence. It is not an accident that across the world, most survivors of sexual violence are women and most perpetrators are men. Sexual encounters are one of the arenas through which power relations are played out. This doesn't mean that sex with men is inherently dangerous for women – what is dangerous is the assumption that sexual violence only occurs because of a lack of understanding of consent and not because men are socialised to constitute themselves and their masculinity through aggressive domination, among a number of other dehumanising practices.

In a world that can be described in the simplest terms as an unequal playing field, there is no 'consensual' interaction that occurs between anyone that is unaffected by power. This does not remove the necessity of consent or suggest that women lack agency in sexual situations. It means, fundamentally, that consent is not easy, or simple. It is a negotiation of the structures that shape our existence. Yes does not always mean yes. 'Yes' might mean, *I am scared for my safety if I say no*. Yes might mean, *I am scared that I'll be penalised in the next assignment if I say no*. Yes might mean, *I'm afraid I will lose my job if I say no*. It is ludicrous to suggest that every 'yes' means that women feel comfortable, safe or that they agree to everything that follows. Understanding consent not as self-evident exchange but as a framework for thinking about the decisions we make refocuses us on what is at stake when we say 'no.' It sharpens our focus, revealing who has the freedom to say no. The burden is often placed on women to define interactions ands set the parameters in which they take place. A more nuanced understanding of consent removes the blame from women who said yes when they meant no or the women who wished they could say no. Viewing consent not as an isolated phenomenon, but as a result of power relations makes it clearer that we do not all have the same social power or mobility. Our 'yeses' and our 'no's' do not carry the same weight.

Perhaps the most dangerous aspect of overly simplistic ideas about consent is how they have been weaponised and misused by feminists to diminish the agency of sex workers – some of the most marginalised women in society. Liberal notions of consent argue that women who provide sexual services in exchange for money cannot possibly consent because, in a patriarchal society, this exchange is devoid of real choice. If we wish to practice a feminism that cares for *all* instead of turning sex workers into enemies of the movement or merely a rhetorical device, then we should all be concerned about how liberal ideas of consent have been weaponised by feminists to push for legislative measures that increase the likelihood that they experience violence, go missing or die. We must refuse the idea that consent is easy. Expressing agency under our current conditions requires a constantly shifting set of negotiations that are not adequately captured by slogans printed on t-shirts, bumper stickers and posters.

Supporting sex workers

'You don't have to like your job to want to keep it.'[2] In their groundbreaking book, *Revolting Prostitutes*, Juno Mac and Molly

---

2   Juno Mac and Molly Smith, *Revolting Prostitutes* (London: Verso, 2018), p. 55.

Smith demonstrate how feminists can support sex workers. The major anti-sex work contention is that sex work cannot be work because it involves sex, and that the sale of sex is worse than the selling of other kinds of labour. Feminist abolitionists of the 80s and 90s likened sex work to rape, arguing that the presence of a transaction negated the ability to consent. This became a powerful rhetorical slogan that suggested that anything other than demands for criminalisation of the sex industry meant approval of sexual violence and trafficking. A number of women's organisations, high profile feminists and MPs have been at the forefront of a decade-long battle to criminalise the buyers of sex and bolster police efforts to crack down on sex workers under the guise of helping more women exit 'prostitution'. They focus on the figure of the 'pimp', a seedy and almost always racialised man who controls the lives of women and forces them to engage in sex work against their will. They want to 'save' women from a deeply exploitative industry by bolstering the carceral state.[3]

Not only does this deeply oversimplify the many ways that women exist in the sex work industry, it uses liberal ideas of 'consent' to make the argument that sex work should be abolished. The argument that women who enter sex work because they have no other choice cannot consent or make decisions ignores the fact that this kind of 'non-decision' is at the very basis of our society. There are a host of decisions that are beyond the individual's control. We don't 'consent' to work, we work because it is necessary for our survival. We don't 'consent' to live under sexist, racist, homophobic structures. We don't 'consent' to have our taxes used to fund wars, but the state may use it in this way if they wish. The world we live in is already a world devoid of choice; it is already coercive by nature. But here the

3   www.dissentmagazine.org/blog/booked-origins-carceral-state-elizabeth-hinton (last accessed 09/2019).

feminist task becomes even clearer: if at the most basic level, consent is the freedom to make decisions, then we must craft a world where those decisions are not governed by oppressive structures. Our focus should be on the structures that push the majority of women into sex work, not individual women who are merely finding ways to survive.

This is why a complicated understanding of consent is so important. Suggesting that sex workers cannot consent is dangerous. It underplays the seriousness and prevalence of sexual violence in the sex work industry, (*if everything is rape, then nothing is rape*) but fundamentally it erases the life-changing decisions that sex workers are forced to make every single day to protect their safety: where to work, who to work with, how to advertise their services. If our understanding of consent recognises that there are power dynamics that shape why and how we consent to specific activities, it becomes clear that poverty does not remove the ability to consent – it merely shapes the decisions sex workers make. If we accept that we do not make any choices that can be neatly separated from the deeply coercive nature of our society, then the argument that sex work is wrong because the women engaged in it cannot exercise free 'choice' begins to fall apart.

Extending solidarity to sex workers means recognising the many ways that the law is stacked against them. Currently in the UK, sex work is partially criminalised. This means that while the sale of sex is legal, there are a host of related 'crimes' that are not: brothel-keeping, curb-crawling, and soliciting in a public place. The Sexual Offences Act 2003 makes it illegal to manage or assist in the management of a brothel. But a 'brothel' is defined as two or more people engaged in sex work working in the same area. This means that sex workers are forced to work alone, in more secretive and shady locations with clients they have not vetted and are unfamiliar with. Criminalisation forces sex workers to make life-threatening decisions every day. Any feminist position that increases the likelihood of death in the workplace is indefensible. Yet 'feminist' parliamentarians and women's NGO's have consistently supported the introduction and extension of criminalisation through the Nordic Model (discussed below), under the guise that this legal framework protects women's well-being.

Sex-worker led groups such as SWARM and The English Collective of Prostitutes have drawn attention to the dangers of this model and its associated consequences for decades. In 2019, The ECP launched a petition calling for the UK government to implement the Home Affairs Committee recommendations that sex work in the UK be decriminalised. SWARM have created and distributed countless resources made by sex workers, which demonstrate that it is impossible to abolish sex work without abolishing the society that creates the need for individuals to sell sex. Across the world, most sex workers are women and most buyers of sex are men. Like every other job, sex work cannot be separated from violent patriarchal structures that create a demand of the sale of sex, from specific bodies, in specific contexts, in particular ways. But by focusing on material conditions, we can recognise that the current conditions under which sex workers are forced to conduct their work by the state are life threatening.

Everyone deserves to be safe

As you read this, women and non-binary sex workers are experiencing high levels of gendered violence at work. In their collection of facts and statistics, The English Collective of Prostitutes found that a global systemic review of violence against sex workers reported that 45–75 per cent of sex workers experienced workplace violence over a lifetime.[4] We are in a moment of crisis.

The forced proximity to violence, law enforcement and incarceration for sex workers cannot and should not be ignored. We don't have to be in love with the sex work industry or its practices in order to make a passionate claim that sex work is work and workers deserve rights. Mac and Smith suggest that while feminists tie themselves in knots about the significations of sex work and its moral implications, women die. 'Rather than focusing on the "work" of sex work, both pro-sex feminists and anti-prostitution feminists concerned themselves with sex as symbol. Both groups questioned what the existence of the sex industry implied for their own positions as women; both groups prioritised those questions over what material improvements could be made in the lives of sex workers in their communities.'[5] The majority of sex workers in the UK are working mothers, who cited the need to pay 'household expenses and support their children' as one of the main reasons for entering the sex work industry.[6]

We know that 86 per cent of austerity cuts have targeted women.[7] If our task is an immediate end to the harm we experience, does it not make sense to begin with ensuring that sex workers do not experience violence at work? We must redirect our attention away from clients and onto the people doing the work, giving them the power to assert their rights, protections and freedoms. Any world without sex work begins with these questions. For too long, sex workers have been turned into a

---

4 http://prostitutescollective.net/2016/11/facts-sex-work/ (last accessed 04/2019).

5 Mac and Smith, *Revolting Prostitutes*, p. 11.

6 http://prostitutescollective.net/2016/11/facts-sex-work (last accessed 04/2019).

7 https://fullfact.org/economy/austerity-women (last accessed 02/2019).

fiction. Narratives of the sex worker as the deviant 'woman' and the 'syphilitic whore' have dominated the public imagination, resulting in our inability to imagine women engaged in sex work alongside their complicated and diverse histories. The victim of 'prostitution' is always a fragile white woman, never a black migrant woman. Never a working-class mother of three. Never young women students struggling to cope with living costs and tuition fees.

To recognise these bodies and voices would mean refusing to foreclose anyone from our feminist protection. It would require us to take a strong stance against border regimes that fuel trafficking, against racism, against policing. To make sex workers real, we must first understand the complex relationship between trafficking and sex work. Some migrants are forced into sex work by traffickers, others cross borders with the intention of selling sex because they know it will provide the most stable income. The government often uses anti-trafficking legislation to detain and deport migrants of all kinds and to crack down on sex workers. Anti-trafficking legislation is anti-migrant insofar as it seeks to reaffirm the permanence of borders and expel the bodies that it marks as illegal. Anti-trafficking legislation and agents who enable it do not care for the well-being of those in the sex industry. When anti-sex work feminists talk about the very real and devastating consequences of trafficking and bolster the police state to respond to it, they do so with the intention of fortifying the borders that ruin people's lives, not with the intention of tearing them down.

The Nordic model

There is no face, or voice that can speak to all sex workers' experiences. Equally, there is not a single voice that proclaims the right course of action to improve the lives of sex workers. Many sex workers who no longer engage with the industry belong to the movements that fight to end sex work through criminalisation. The criminalisation of sex workers, better known as the Nordic model first enacted in Sweden, is often referred to by abolitionists as a desire to 'end demand.' It criminalises the buying of sex but not the selling of sex. The rationale of this model sees that women who sell sex should not be penalised for doing so, but instead provided with resources to 'exit' the sex work industry. It uses a moralising logic to claim that because the sex work industry is inherently exploitative it should be abolished, whilst simultaneously leaving all other exploitative industries intact. But criminalisation of buyers means penalisation for sex workers.

We do not currently live in a society that could support the abolition of sex work. To create such a society would require a complete transformation of social structures. Even if such a society existed, 'sex work' as we know it would take on a new set of meanings. It might not necessarily disappear. But the immediate needs of sex workers, the urgency of their deaths as a result of criminalisation should outweigh the desires of middle class feminists who have never worried about the cost of living. The reality of the situation wakes us up to the immediate danger we place women in when feminists advocate for criminalisation on their behalf. The idea that women need to be 'rescued' from the industry stems from a dangerous and misguided idea that the law brings salvation. Policemen are not saviours, and as we have discussed throughout the book, we clearly cannot rely on the state to deliver justice. The idealist approach behind the Nordic model forcefully clashes with the reality of our lived situations. It turns the difference between life and death into a dangerous game. Criminalisation of the buyers of sex makes it harder for sex workers to find clients. This model traps women who enter the sex work industry out of desperation by forcing them to push their work underground to attract clients who do not want to risk going to prison. That means entering unmarked cars, having sex in unfamiliar locations, not vetting clients, increasing the likelihood of being assaulted because you need to become untraceable in order to work.

It makes it easier for sex workers to go missing, as is the case with Anneli Alderton, Paula Clennel, Gemma Adams, Tania Nicol, Annette Nicholls, Christina Abbotts, Daria Pionko. The 'missing' sex worker quickly becomes the dead sex worker, usually at the hands of a male client. Criminalising sex work does nothing to end the urgency of this situation. It facilitates the detention of vulnerable women who end up in prison for working together and sanctions police raids under the guise of 'rescuing' women such as the raid in Soho in 2013, which left many women homeless and led to forced removals of migrant sex workers in the UK.[8] Over and over again, when sex workers in the industry have unionised, when they have formed collectives, they have demanded decriminalisation as the most freeing legal context in which sex work can exist. Even if we cannot know intimately what it means to be a sex worker, we know violence. We bear witness to it in our everyday lives and so, when sex workers speak, we are called to listen.

Legalisation versus decriminalisation

Decriminalisation differs from the legalisation of sex work and the Nordic model because it places power back into the hands of those selling sex to determine where their work takes place, how it takes place and the means through which they negotiate

---

8   Mac and Smith, *Revolting Prostitutes*.

with clients. The legalisation of sex work relegates these decisions to the state. In Germany and states like Nevada in the USA, selling sex is legal. The problem with this model is that, when the state 'regulates' sex work, it places bureaucratic restrictions on sex workers by deciding where they work, how they work, forces them to undergo mandatory sexual health testing and stipulates the terms of their employment. But what if you're poor and can't afford to comply with strict regulations? You end up being criminalised. Legalisation creates a two-tier system, the happy face of legalised prostitution and the 'unhappy' face of deviant sex workers, who perform their work underground in increasingly unsafe environments because they cannot comply with regulations.

Decriminalisation is a legal model that does not enforce carceral penalties on the sex work industry, ensuring the selling of sex and the purchasing of sex is not illegal. It means that third parties – such as landlords and managers – are not at risk of imprisonment and allows sex workers to access labour law in order to bargain for rights that might protect them from exploitation. The sale of commercial sex moves outside the bounds of criminal law into commercial law. This means, like all other forms of work, the selling of sex is subject to the same laws around coercion, bullying and assault. The most popular example of this model is New Zealand where the Prostitution Reform Act came into force in 2003, due to extensive campaigning from New Zealand's leading sex work organisation, the New Zealand Prostitutes Collective. Not only have studies shown that sex workers reported increased agency in contexts where decriminalisation occurred,[9] decriminalisation is the only legal framework that provides a starting point for thinking about how other forms of criminalised behaviour (drugs, migra-

9   www.otago.ac.nz/christchurch/otago018607.pdf (last accessed 04/2019).

tion) interact with sex work. If sex work is not illegal but drug taking is, what do we do with sex workers who use drugs? If sex work is not illegal, but crossing the border is, what do we do with migrant sex workers who are deemed to be living 'illegally?' There is no 'one size fits all' solution. Advocating for decriminalisation requires us to think beyond the limits of the law; it signals our commitment to making the world a more liveable place. It is a starting point.

As feminists, our concerns should be about more than whether or not sex workers can 'consent' or how commercial sex changes what we know about sex. There is more at stake in this conversation; one thing that those across the spectrum of the debate can agree on is that no woman should be subjected to violence, at any time, in any place. The methods of achieving this reality differ greatly, and are often driven by specific political agendas. Often, so-called 'radical' feminists have teamed up with the Christian Right to proclaim the evils of sex work. But anyone engaged in movements trying to transform society must weigh up the world we want with the world we have. A more expansive idea of consent recognises that though we cannot escape oppressive structures, we do have a certain level of agency within them. While that agency is not freedom, it might mean the difference between eating and going hungry, escaping conflict or staying to die. If we remove the lens of victimhood and view sex workers as capable of making decisions in their best interests and knowing what will make their lives and their work easier, the demand for decriminalisation becomes more than just a demand. It becomes a necessity; a building block for a just society, one where sex work as we know it no longer exists, but transformative sexual relations do. In the meantime, this demand helps us craft a world where women will not have to go to work afraid they might be dead by the end of the week.

Chapter 8

The answer to sexual violence is not more prisons

> For example, in what sense could we produce knowledge about women in prison? . . . This is not merely a question about how we have to rethink knowledge but about how we rethink an abolitionist politics that start from the position of those women on the underside of capital but does not put them in another cage. – Gina Dent[1]

'Upskirting', the practice of taking unauthorised photographs under a person's clothing without their permission, became a criminal offence punishable by up to two years in prison on 12 April 2019. Spearheaded by Gina Martin, the campaign to introduce the bill focused heavily on the 'no-brainer' nature of criminalising this offence. Gina tells the story of having indecent images taken of her at a festival and calling the police, only to be told that, as the act was not a criminal offence, nothing could be done. She did the first thing that many of us are taught to do when things go wrong – turn to the police. Everything about the

---

1 Angela Davis and Gina Dent, 'Prison as a Border: A conversation on Gender, Globalisation and Punishment,' Signs 26, no. 4 (summer): 1235–42.

world we live in tells us that the police are there to protect us and prisons force the criminal to reflect on their actions, deter them from committing other crimes and remind them that nobody is above the law. Here, the wrongdoer, the thief, the rapist, the abuser *deserves* punishment – deserves to experience the pain and suffering that they have put others through. But what about the woman with insecure immigration status for whom calling the police might mean deportation? What about the women from communities for whom police presence has meant the unexplained deaths in custody of their family members? What about sex workers who face sexual violence and harassment from police officers themselves? Realising that the police and law enforcement do not equal safety for everyone is the first step to rethinking ideas about justice.

The idea that justice is served when criminals go to prison is relatively new. In the sixteenth and seventeenth century, 'criminals' were punished using public tools of humiliation, which included whipping, the ducking stool and the pillory. They were killed in public executions. Ironically, prisons were introduced in order to make punishment more 'humane'. They were popularised in the eighteenth century and rarely used; some convicts were shipped to British colonies and required to perform hard labour.[2] The history of prisons is inseparable from the history of the British imperial endeavour. Because of the increased securitisation of our everyday lives, it can seem like prisons and the police have existed forever. We see adverts to join the police force on the London Underground; we see police officers roaming the streets. We learn about the police force in school, and in popular media. Their presence subtly reaffirms the importance of their role in maintaining order. But order for whom and at what cost?

---

2   https://howardleague.org/history-of-the-penal-system (last accessed 05/2019).

Any mother, sister, aunt, cousin, friend who has lost someone to the prison system knows that prisons eat people up. People are removed from society and subjected to inhumane conditions, stifling any chance for them to reintegrate into society once they have been released – countless studies prove that many ex-prisoners go on to re-offend due to lack of employment, housing and social prospects. But the idea that prisons equal justice and that the law is fairly applied is so insidious that mainstream feminist movements turn to these forces as a response to sexual and gendered violence. If we can only imagine justice being served in one way, then carceral responses to sexual violence seem like common sense. The logic is as follows: if we make a law about it, the problem will go away or at the very least, the frequency of the problem will decrease because criminals will know that they can no longer get away with it. But the problem with sexual violence is that no amount of retribution can stem the consequences of an invasion of bodily autonomy. We know that the majority of rapists in the world are not in prison, nor will they ever be. They are walking among us, they are our family members, our friends, they hold government positions; they make the laws they claim will hold others to account.

Whether or not prison brings peace of mind to individual victims, it does not prevent that same violence from being enacted on somebody else. Prison provides an individualistic response to harm – it locates the problem in the body of the 'bad' person rather than connecting patterns of harm to the conditions in which we live. A feminist conceptualisation of justice recognises that the world is organised in ways that expose some women to disproportionate levels of violence. Ironically, the more that liberal feminists invite law enforcement into our homes, schools and civic life looking for protection, the more we place women on the margins (poor, black, trans, disabled) in

amount of legislation or prison sentences can undo the idea that takes root in every young girl's mind as soon as she recognises that she is vulnerable: *I am not safe*. Prisons do nothing for women clutching their keys in the dark on their way home. Surely, a feminist future is one without the need to protect ourselves from harm. A feminist future is a future without sexual violence of any kind. Getting there requires us to stop considering solutions to harm after it has happened and instead turn our attention to thinking about how to prevent harm.

In the UK, the majority of known instances of sexual harassment, assault and rape are carried out by men against women.[6] Anyone who refuses to naturalise aggression, domination and violence in men's bodies, understands that these traits have more to do with enforcement of gender as a system than individual action. Gendered violence is a systemic problem that requires a collective response. It is crucial that we disrupt normative masculinity and the systems it is predicated on before they become cemented in the bodies of individuals. There are a number of ways men might be held accountable, ones that recognise the failure of punitive solutions to change cycles of violence. By refusing to pathologise men's behaviour, feminist responses can also recognise that anybody is capable of harm; the perpetration of sexual violence is not exclusive to men. Oppressive ideas of sex and sexuality come to define every single one of our interactions, no matter who we are.

Carceral responses to sexual violence fail to address the root causes of the problem. Putting an offender in jail does nothing to reshape the logic of sexual and gendered violence, nor does it signal that the act itself was an injustice. Simply criminalising sexual offences will not bring about the wholesale transforma-

6   www.ons.gov.uk/aboutus/transparencyandgovernance/freedomofinformation foi/rapestatisticsbygenderofvictimandperpetrator (last accessed 05/2019).

tion of society that feminism seeks. It simply pushes out the undesirables, filters them from society and then reintroduces them without the means or resources to stop them reoffending.

Abolition feminism

When we speak of prison abolition, the fear of a world without order springs to mind. The idea is that without prisons, without institutions that enforce law and order, there would be no way of keeping us safe. But the logic of prison abolition asks us to interrogate who 'we' are and why we place our safety in opposition to those we imagine place us in danger. Who are *they*? The 'bad' people who become defined by their criminality or the violence they have enacted and can never escape it? Why is it easier to organise a society around the idea that some people deserve to be disappeared into the prison system, while others deserve freedom and the ability to live, work and build a life? The idea that prisons keep those on the outside 'safe' presupposes that they are effective in catching 'bad guys' and putting them away. A belief in prisons presupposes that they are racially neutral, efficient deterrents – that they help rehabilitate criminals and put right the injustice suffered by victims.

Developed by leading pioneers, activists and scholars including Angela Davis, Gina Dent and Ruth Gilmore, abolition feminism asks us to focus on the root causes of the problems that plague our society. Abolition feminism is a feminist theory and practice that seeks a world beyond prisons, offering grassroots solutions to the problems of racism, inadequate mental health support, domestic violence and organising for economic, racial and gender justice. Abolition feminism recognises the harm that prisons do, and how they lead to unnecessary and unavoidable death. It does not trust the state to deliver us justice. Instead of being preoccupied with the question of reform, it cuts right through to the heart of violence. It organises to build a world where prisons are not necessary. This means tackling the issues that put people in prison in the first place: racism, borders, drug use, petty fines. It argues for culturally competent, fully funded mental health services where they were most needed and for the decriminalisation of sex work and drug use. It trains mental health professionals and community members to intervene in violent situations and deescalate them before a 'crime' is committed. It is attentive to the concerns of communities, seeking to expand benefit, housing, social services, healthcare and education systems, engaging in political education and instilling a radical feminist ethos into every single person that comes under our care and protection. It campaigns against prison expansion, stop and search and mandatory conviction targets, fights the gutting of vital youth services, as well as all overt and covert methods of criminalisation.

Abolition begins with an end to prison expansion, a fight against the privatisation of prisons and the immediate release of all political prisoners. Abolition feminism begins at home – it resists the desire to catastrophise (*what do we do with all the murderers?*) and realises that murder is not only uncommon in many contexts but is also entirely avoidable. It focuses on how we might create the conditions to transform the relations that cause crime in the first place. It asks us to identify the areas where our communities are sick and suffering and to propose solutions that do not involve detention, restriction, sectioning, policing. It asks us not to call 999 on somebody who is vulnerable and could be helped in another way and recognises that prisons merely wrap dirty gauze around dirty wounds; they reinfect our society every moment they stay open.

Prison expansion

In November 2016, the British government released a white paper that stated its commitment to create 10,000 new prison places, through the construction of six megaprisons and five new 'residential centres' for women. Corporate Watch stated that five of those were to be completed by 2020. Despite the government abandoning some of these plans, it remains vital to explore how women offenders and victims are mobilised in debates around prison expansion. Gender has become central to the justification of the building and expansion of our Prison Island. There are reports that the Scottish government is considering building a new prison to hold non-binary people in order to '[increase] the protections against discrimination on the basis of a person's gender identity.'[7]

While this plan may appear to some as a sensitive move on the part of the government to respond to conversations about gender in society, for critical feminists, it provides further justification to divorce feminism from the state apparatus and put forward a new vision for what justice could look like. There is no such thing as a socially conscious prison. Prisons are by their very nature, oppressive. The things that we care about – sexual assault, rape, domestic violence – are used by the state to justify harsher prison sentences and the expansion of the prison industrial complex across the world. The advocates of this expansion do not care about ending violence; they care about prisons as for-profit entities and as places where the labour of prisoners can be exploited. If we know that the existence of prisons has no real impact on rates for reoffending, that abuse, self-harm and

---

7   https://corporatewatch.org/new-non-binary-prison-in-scotland (last accessed 05/2019).

suicide are rife in prisons[8] and that, in the cases of sexual assault and rape, individuals are very unlikely to go to prison in the first place, it becomes clear that the safety that carceral thinking sells us is a lie.

Feminists fight back

In 2017, Sisters Uncut occupied the Visitors Centre of Holloway Prison and held a week long festival of community events to highlight the potential of the space to be used as a vehicle for community building and care. When they occupied Holloway, they did not know what the space could be, but they entered with the hope of reclamation. A member of Sisters Uncut told me:

We wanted to show that safe spaces for the community are needed for our learning, healing, and support. That it's possible to create a transformative space even in a place so historically saturated in violence . . . During the occupation, the whole space was decorated with home-made bunting and curtains, tablecloths, cushions with slogans 'CARE NOT CAGES' and 'SAFETY IS A RIGHT' knitted onto the covers, and a pink banner that said 'This is a political occupation' in sparkling letters. Much of the decor was purple and green, the Sisters colours. Not just the physical space, but the whole atmosphere was transformed. The smell of delicious food being cooked throughout the day, sitting and eating meals together, painting each other's nails or drawing and craft-making with the kids; it was no doubt a very different vibe from the old visitors centre.

---

8   www.theguardian.com/society/2019/jan/31/prison-figures-reveal-rise-in-deaths-assaults-and-self-harm (last accessed 05/2019).

The work of reclaiming the space did not end when the festival ended. Sisters Uncut are calling for private property developers that now own the land that the prison is built on to commit to building genuinely affordable housing and a women's building after its demolition. Sisters Uncut oppose prisons in disguise, so called 'residential women's centres' funded by the state that seek to put a glossier face on incarceration. They want the site of the largest women's prison in Europe, to become something else – another place for women to come together.

> We are trying to arrange meetings with Peabody, who own the land now, to find out what their plans are so far for the women's centre and to present them with our own plans of our vision for the space . . . I am worried about Peabody's interpretation of 'women's centre,' and hope that we can apply pressure both as local community stakeholders through building that relationship with Peabody and also publicly, by writing articles and creating media around the site with actions and demos . . . In June 2018, the MOJ announced that they were 'scrapping' plans to build 5 women's prisons. However, with this same announcement came one instead about opening 5 'residential centres'. While we don't have much information on the locations of these new centres or how they will be run, a project that is still run and funded by the MOJ and within a system wherein vulnerable people are criminalised before being provided with support services does nothing to dismantle the framework of criminal justice and punishment.

Activist efforts are also at risk of being co-opted by the state. Prisons under another name do not spell freedom. In the UK, groups like Empty Cages, CAPE, Women in Prison and INQUEST have furthered the fight for prison abolition. They spread information, skill share and work directly with communities affected by the prison industrial complex in the UK. They expose the increasingly privatised nature of the prison industry, the prevalence of the school to prison pipeline, and the fact that the UK has the most privatised prison system in Europe, with 11.6 per cent of the total prison population being held in a private prison.[9] But prison as a profit-making endeavour is not new – state-owned prisons have always been moneymakers. Private companies provide the food and maintenance services that keep prisons going. There at 14 private prisons in the UK, which hold one fifth of all UK prisoners and are run by three companies: G4S Justice Services, SodexoJustice Services and Serco Custodial Services. Private prisons mean that corporations can generate profit from those in prisons, putting them to work to produce goods that can be bought and sold on the outside. This bolsters the intricate systems, networks and relationships between prisons, the police, the probation service, courts and all of the companies that profit from the movement and containment of individuals.

If corporations can make money from prisoners, then incarceration is just another mode through which the logic of capital structures the way society is organised. This for-profit motive is aided by globalisation: private companies build prisons across the world, reproducing colonial era style methods of extraction and labour production. There are American owned prisons in Australia, Kenya and South Africa. Perhaps the most dangerous part of prison is the fact that we do not really know what happens on the inside. Whether prisoners' labour is exploited or not, whether they are left with little to do to stimulate their mind or

---

9 www.prisonabolition.org/what-is-the-prison-industrial-complex (last accessed 05/2019).

aid the process of 'rehabilitation' – prisons are a private endeavour; they seek to isolate and insulate. They cut off connection.

Feminism and transformative justice

The principles of transformative justice offer us a challenge. Instead of relying on the law, prison and police to rectify the harm committed by an individual, we undergo a process of community accountability. A group of friends, a church, an organisation come together and design a process to hold an individual to account without sending them away. This process might look like: community service, reflective practice, reaffirming commitment to values and practices, mediation, finding methods to cope with rage and shame, therapy, mental health support and trauma-centred programmes designed to identify the root causes of behaviour. In the case of sexual violence, often the criminal justice system can re-traumatise victims and survivors, asking them to rehash evidence of the violence inflicted upon them, subjecting them to cross-examination and to the scrutiny of the public.

A transformative justice approach would not only be attentive to the needs of survivors and victims, it would lift the burden of proof that lay with them. What transformative justice offers, is the specificity that rectifying instances of harm may require. It is not a broad-brush approach but rather a tailor made process designed for specific individuals. Perhaps one of the most chilling realisations is that for some offences, there can be no adequate punishment. No punishment can completely undo the multi-layered consequences of harm – so crafting methods of harm reduction and prevention is not only a feminist response to crime; it is the only response that does not reproduce the violence it seeks to eradicate. When prison abolition is referred to as 'utopian' it signals to the public imagination that we do not currently possess the resources to make that vision a reality. Not only is this untrue, it stifles our ability to take the necessary steps towards prison abolition. Across the world, activist groups are preventing the building of new prisons, establishing political education for prisoners and forging links between those on the inside and those on the outside. Abolitionist work is happening all around us, we only have to look for it.

Justice means everyone. If feminist work is justice work, it must be able to stand up to the complexities of our lives. We are too messy to be divided into 'good' and 'bad' people, the former deserving of freedom and the latter deserving of cruelty. Feminism seeks to give us back the ability to care and relate to one another in ways we have yet to imagine. Feminism responds to urgency, and prisons pose one of the most urgent questions of our time: What kind of world would we like to live in?

Chapter 9

Feminism and food

In the 1970s, food was a feminist issue and I was a fat feminist. Always looking for a quasi politically correct excuse to eat. – Faith Ringgold, performance story quilt

Women are stuck in their bodies. Constantly haunted by what they look like, what they don't look like, how they should look and how we can change them. Received wisdom tells us that social media is worsening our perception of ourselves and distorting reality. The ability to manipulate facial and bodily features: make ourselves thinner, fatter, darker, lighter and erase all that we deem imperfect is bound to make having a body a complicated affair. But, the anxiety of wanting to be beautiful, of having a body, of *watching what you eat* is nothing new; social media didn't create it. It is present at the dinner table, in the words of the family member who chides you when you go up for a second helping. Bodies bear the marks of the world we live in: gendered, racialised, sexualised. The socio-economic consequences of the work we do, what we eat and how much we get to rest takes its toll on us. For women, there is something sinister about how every part of our public and private worlds is deeply invested in making us doubt that our bodies are enough as they are. From dieting adverts on YouTube, Instagram and Facebook, to the state dictating that children be weighed as part of the

National Child Measurement Programme, an initiative that seeks to monitor signs of obesity in children as young as four, numbers follow us around. The scale is a dreaded instrument that shows us plain as day, that we are not doing our lives right.

In July 2019, Cancer Research UK, fundraising partners with dieting organisation *Slimming World*, launched a multi-million pound campaign using defunct scientific indicators to claim that obesity was the second leading cause of cancer. Adverts appeared on tubes, buses and billboards. This scaremongering has become so routine that it goes unquestioned. After all, the worst thing to be as a young woman is too much: too loud, too opinionated or too *big*. It is no coincidence that the majority of people with eating disorders are young girls. Food controls us, and most women feel this from an early age. Women's bodies have always been the property of everyone but themselves. If most eating disorders are driven by a need for control, then they cannot be detached from societies that are built on the leveraging of young women's agency from the moment they are born. The desire to be smaller is driven and has always been driven by a fear of fatness. To be fat is to be despised: to have the world made harder to move around in, to be scorned and derided, to not be able to find clothes or bras to fit your body, to pay extra for a plane seat. More seriously: to be denied healthcare because you refuse to lose weight and to die because of that denial. Fat people are more likely to die than their thinner counterparts, not because of their bodies, but because our entire healthcare system is bolstered by anti-fat stigma and discrimination.[1] Heart problems? Lose weight. Cancer? Lose weight. Want to be eligible for life-changing surgery? You have to lose weight. To be fat is

---

1   https://bmcobes.biomedcentral.com/articles/10.1186/s40608-015-0064-2 (last accessed 08/2019).

to be considered a drain on the nation's resources and perhaps most damning of all: to be ugly.

Having a body is stressful when it could be easy. There is no clearer manifestation of neo-liberalism than in our attitudes towards bodies. If you do not have the right kind of body, you cannot be the perfect worker – neo-liberalism turns us into units of production whose value is measured by what we can individually achieve. This kind of thinking is written all over our bodies: for as long as we have lived, our economies have largely depended on forms of manual labour. With increasing moves towards automation, it's even harder to work. We're stressed, out-sourced, on zero-hour contracts, in competition with machines. In this world, fat bodies signify a kind of moral deviance, a refusal to fall in line. Where fatness was originally associated with the rich, who overindulged and lived without limits, it is increasingly becoming a sign of working class neglect. Fatness is associated with rising 'cost' under a regime where human life is measured quantitatively. To be fat means to be more expen-sive to look after because more resources are needed to care for you. More time is needed. This attempt to compartmentalise human life and to measure it according to cost-benefit analysis has seeped down into the social and political policy that governs the way we live.

The most recent and damning example of this in the UK is the introduction of the sugar tax. From 6 April 2018, manufacturers were required by law to lower the sugar content in drinks or pay a levy that would raise the price of fizzy drinks by 18 pence per litre on drinks that have more than 5g of sugar per 100ml, or 24 pence per litre on those with more than 8g of sugar per 100ml. The sugar tax was long fought for by 'anti-obesity' cam-paigners, who argued that its introduction would help tackle the number of fat children in the UK and lessen the likelihood of fat adults who drain NHS resources. This exposes that the motivation behind the tax was linked to the economic consequences of caring for fat people. Instead of lowering sugar content, most manufacturers have opted to change their recipes, using substitutes for sugar that do nothing to change nutritional value.

So often, anxieties about what is 'healthy' mask systematic disdain for fat bodies. Instead of debunking the myth that fatness means ill health by regurgitating scientific studies, it is perhaps more urgent to consider the way a hatred of fatness and a society premised on aggressive individualism work to reinforce one another. In other words, the world we live in is unhealthy, not the bodies that inhabit it. Under the guise of concerns about 'health', the government has sanctioned the policing of certain types of drinks – those consumed by the poorest in society. The logic of scarcity that underpins this move wishes to decrease our reliance on social systems of care: it sees people using the benefit system or healthcare or social services as liabilities to be curtailed. This logic is not only cruel and dehumanising, it threatens a radical feminist future. In an ideal world, we might treasure these systems as mechanisms that help us live longer, fuller and more pleasurable lives. The point would be to use them because it is okay to rely on something other than yourself. When neo-liberalism quantifies human life using the language of burden and responsibility, it chips away at an ethos of collectivity, one that recognises that we have more than enough resources in the world we live in to care for all.

The dinner table

On the commute home from work, mothers across the country are already thinking about what to make for dinner. For the poorest women, often this thought process is filled with anxiety.

They do not have the luxury of considering nutritional value: of mulling over and picking the foods that might be best for their child's development or health. The demands on their body and time mean they can only think about what will fill their stomachs. Maybe they're counting coins, maybe they are thinking about how best to utilise the last can of beans from the food bank. Nearly half of single parents in the UK – working or unemployed – live in relative poverty. The poorest women are trapped in low paid, insecure work often without benefits or security; every area of their lives and their children's lives are affected.

If you are poor or have ever been poor, you understand that food is about much more than what you eat. It is the difference between women able to buy fresh produce straight from a supplier and women who skip meals to ensure that their kids do not go hungry. Research by the Food Foundation found that 4 million children in the UK live in households that would struggle to afford to buy enough fruit, vegetables and fish to meet 'official' nutrition guidelines.[2] While it is right to question the purpose of 'nutritional guidelines' and to understand that health is a complex, shifting and ever-changing idea, inequalities in access to different kinds of food are stark. Low-income households are more likely to be concentrated in inner-city areas inhabited by black people and people of colour. The fast-food shops that line the corners of inner city areas are political agents. The differences in air quality, road safety and the number of open and accessible green spaces in each borough are not merely a matter of chance. When feminists proclaim that poorer women have a lower quality of life, they mean that just by virtue of where they live, they are already more likely to die prematurely. When

2 https://foodfoundation.org.uk/new-report-on-the-affordability-of-a-healthy-diet (last accessed: 08/ 2019).

we begin to think about food outside the realm of what we as individuals 'choose' to put in our bodies and instead consider the political factors that shape which foods we can access, it becomes clear that food is a feminist issue.

Often, single parent households headed by women are demonised for the rise in childhood obesity rates – this fatphobic narrative scolds mothers for the lack of attention to their children's diets. News and media outlets drum up a moral panic about children getting *fat* – reaffirming the idea that to be fat is to be wrong just by virtue of existing. The association between fatness and lazy parenting makes clear that the former should be avoided at all costs. It signals to fat women and girls that their bodies exist as evidence of lack of education, due diligence and care. But the government focus on 'lowering obesity' does little to address the way that poverty limits our nutritional choices. A feminist approach to food recognises that the aim is not to eradicate fatness, but to undo the conditions that cause a disparity in our access to different kinds of food. Nobody has a monopoly on what is healthy. To pretend as if there were a single received wisdom about what a 'healthy' diet or lifestyle is, is to completely ignore how relative the concept of health is.

The conditions that we live in affect everything: from what we eat, to how we prepare it to how we present it. Living in a deeply oppressive society robs us of the ability to think about food as nourishment. To be nourished means to be brimful, satisfied and to treat our bodies with loving-kindness. Nourishment is the opposite of policing and gatekeeping. Nourishment rejects any attempt to blame us for our bodies, to shame us for what we look like or the food we eat. Nourishment rejects dieting. Nourishment is a feminist project because for too long, women's bodies and what they consume have been monitored. Women are blamed if their children eat too much or too little, if they eat the wrong kind of food or if they stop eating altogether. Food is something we need to survive, but all of the pleasure of food – of making meals, of sharing them with the ones we love – is tainted by surroundings that dictate that food is fuel and fuel keeps us going, ensuring that we can work and continue to be productive. 'Food as fuel' leads to diets based on necessity: stripped back, bland meals packed with protein, consumed quickly and without ceremony. This keeps many women trapped in a cycle of eating, but never *tasting*.

Body positivity mantras inform us that we should view food not as the enemy, but as a source of energy because it makes our body do things. We should be grateful that food makes our arms, legs and brains work. But this mantra falls short by treating action as the only positive outcome of consumption. It rests on the idea that we should be grateful for food not just because it exists, but because of what it does for our bodies. It treats bodies as if they were merely vehicles for action and not ambivalent, changing houses for the things that make us human. Rethinking the relationship between our bodies and the food we eat means rejecting the logic of functionality. Because of the way our societies are built, our bodies fail us all the time, so does the food we eat.

What if our bodies are chronically ill? What if food does not give us energy? What if the food we eat makes us sick? What if our bodies turn against us? What if they get us killed? In a different world, we might eat for the sake of eating: smell, taste, touch and really take time to get to know our ingredients. Feminism is interested in finding new ways to make our lives worth living and while things like food and fashion have often been dismissed as frivolous, they are modes of expression. One day, we might be freer to use food to tell stories about ourselves: our cultures, histories, and memories. A liberated future means a future predicated on pleasure: more love, more good meals shared together in new and exciting ways. But in order to achieve this, there must be a wholesale rethinking of food: from identifying the unjust labour practices that produce ingredients, the labour that is involved in preparing food and the role of food production in climate catastrophe. Across the world, women's lives are implicated in food production and distribution in life-threatening and exploitative ways. If food is a feminist issue, the fight is not just about what our meals should taste like.

Women's work

Food preparation and distribution is most often women's work. Women routinely shop for food ingredients, prepare meals and ensure that their families and partners are well fed and cared for. This work is often mind numbingly boring. Women's domestic labour has always been overlooked, downplayed or invisibilised. Often the desire to cook food is essentialised: we are told that women produce food for their families as a demonstration of love. Though this may be true, it erases the labour that makes this act of love possible. Often the labour that goes into this act of care: cutting vegetables, acquiring spices, washing the necessary utensils is not viewed as real 'work' or compensated. Preparing meals is not work in the same way that fixing a car is, or filing reports or building a house, though it is crucial to the functioning of entire households and economies.

In the 1970s, Wages for Housework campaigns emerged across the world. They made an international demand: that all carers be paid for the work that took place inside the home. Spearheaded by women such as Selma James, Silvia Federeci and Mariposa Dalla Costa, Italian autonomists, the movement sought to redefine domestic care work as work and transform exploitative relations of power through the demand for a wage for care workers. They argued that the domestic sphere was political and made clear that marriage, pregnancy and mothering were contingent on the enforcement of extractive social and political arrangements. Wages for Housework represented an entirely new approach to understanding the tenants of 'wife' and 'mother', including all of the unpaid labour they performed out of 'love'. However flawed the movement was – black feminists argued that the demand did not take into account their centuries of paid domestic labour and that demanding to be paid for work is not the same as demanding that nobody is forced to perform dull domestic labour – it is evidence of the ways feminists have refused to let the 'little' things: cooking, cleaning, caring, go unrecognised. When we understand the patterns of exploitation that underpin the way our households are run – cooking and eating take on entirely new meanings. Every meal cooked by a mother or a carer within the home is inextricably bound up in the cycles of power and exploitation that keep our world going. The private sphere has never just been private. When we eat, we must eat acknowledging the work that goes into making the meal as well as the luxury in preparing it with relative ease, while many women around the world go hungry.

Food is about land, too

Berta Careres was assassinated in her home by armed intruders on 22 March 2016, two days before her forty-fifth birthday. She coordinated grassroots protests to halt the construction of a hydroelectric dam on the Gualcarque river, held sacred by the Lenca people. Seven men were convicted for her murder, ordered by executives of the Agua Zarca Dam company. She is one of the many Indigenous women fighting resource extraction that have lost their lives protecting land that is central to the communities they live in. Resisting climate crisis, land grabs and the destruction of dams, wells, clean water supplies and harvesting fields is central to indigenous ways of living. Listening to the land, understanding its history and refusing to subordinate land to human interest are ideas that are deeply embedded in feminist Indigenous resistance. Land matters because indigenous lives are being systematically eradicated. In Canada, Indigenous women are being disappeared by the state at alarming rates, are most likely to experience violence at the hands of non-natives and become prime targets from hitmen and multinational corporations because they are a core component of resistance movements opposing the destruction of their livelihoods.

As feminists, if we care about the food we eat, we must also care about the contexts in which that food is produced and the ways that production attacks our ways of living. The destruction of land via oil pipelines and other forms of pollution affects crops and the quality of life of the women and families who are slowly poisoned. In order to cultivate a more holistic approach to understanding food, ideas of land and labour practices must be central to our feminisms. Recognising the multiple dimensions of an issue is always also an attempt to recognise the interconnected and overlapping elements of our lives. The deep-rooted inequalities in the way we eat in the West and the working class families that are most harshly affected by them are inextricably linked to the struggles for ownership of land waged by Indigenous communities in the Americas and elsewhere.

In the US, the majority of the agricultural sector is powered by the labour of undocumented migrants who often have no choice but to enter the farming industry to earn the money they need to live. In Europe, current migration patterns reveal that the most frequent movements between borders are from asylum seekers. Italy and Spain have the greatest number of migrant women in the agricultural sector.[3] Across continents, the story is the same. Without proper protections in place, these workers can be subjected to any manner of exploitative practices: from physical abuse to sexual violence with no recourse for justice. Often working in gruelling conditions in high temperatures: the work impacts their bodies, minds and spirits. So, food is also about borders, about how the food we eat is a major site where some of the most devastating power relations are played out. A feminist response requires us to think about ways to lessen the violence borders create on the journey to abolishing them. Joining anti-raid networks, lying down in front of charter flights, offering to house those with insecure immigration status are all first steps. As feminists, it is important to support and extend the right to unionise for migrants, make it easier for people to move between nations and subvert the fortress that has been built around Europe.

Across the world, women are the backbone of rural farming communities; they are responsible for 60–80 per cent of food production in the Global South.[4] If women's labour is central to the maintenance of global economies, then our feminism is purposeless if it doesn't endeavour to expose the extent of the ill treatment they experience in their everyday lives. It would be unwise to adopt a way of thinking that sees us living our lives in isolation. Building global demands about the food we eat means recognising that freedom from the tyranny of our own body image and beauty standards is not possible without a just

3 www.europarl.europa.eu/RegData/etudes/STUD/2018/604966/IPOL_STU (2018)604966_EN.pdf (last accessed 05/2019).

4 www.fao.org/3/am307e/am307e00.pdf (last accessed 05/2019).

system of food production. It might follow that in a world where our food was manufactured, prepared and presented without exploitation, where everyone had enough to eat and recipes to nourish them, food would cease to be the enemy for so many young girls. The good food that awaits us in the future requires us all to be at the table.

Chapter 10

Solidarity is a doing word

We the women of the YPJ, the women's self-defence militias, salute all the women fighters of Latin America. We want these women to know that we are not just taking up a military struggle against ISIS but that also one of the main goals of our struggle is to create a new society where women are free. We want to express our support for the right of all women to free, safe, and legal abortion. As Kurdish women, we are closely following your struggle. Not one more woman dead due to a back-alley abortion! ¡Jin Jian Azadi! – Women, life and freedom! – YPJ, Women's Protection Units

حرية سلام و عدالة و الثورة خيار الشعب, (Freedom, peace, justice . . . the revolution is the choice of the people) – Sudanese Revolution Chant

We climb the mountain in our ways, towards the same summit. As we continue in our respective ways to resist the Hong Kong Police Force, the summit of our imagining may well emerge the form of a new, anti-carceral collective – Jun Pang

Solidarity has always been at the heart of feminist practice. Ideas of 'global sisterhood' rose to prominence in the late twentieth century, its advocates called for the need to view women's liberation across borders and continents. Although this relied on the flawed concept of a 'universal patriarchy', it opened up space to consider the power of refusing to remain divided by something as arbitrary as geographical location. What has always underpinned radical feminist movements is the global nature of their demands and their ability to understand the interlocking nature of structures of oppression. Perhaps one of the most galvanising instances of international solidarity in recent history was inspired by the arrest and detainment of the black political revolutionary Angela Davis, falsely charged in connection with the murder of Judge Harold Haley in 1970. Feminist groups from across the world called for her release through letters, statements and acts of solidarity. These groups included: The National Union of Mexican Women, The Angolan Women's Committee, Somali women in Mogadishu, The Egyptian Women's Committee and Guyana's Women's Progressive Organisation. In this instance, the feminist collectives that practiced transformational politics understood what was lost when movements isolated themselves and made demands only within the boundaries of nation states.

Solidarity breaks down the concept of the nation or the idea that the world and the many countries it contains are not linked by present and historical networks of exploitation, colonial rule and military alliances. The work of knowing what is happening in the complex puzzle that is the world, means acknowledging the struggles that occur parallel and adjacent to our own. Often, the demands feminists make in their respective countries are the same. In Ireland, STRIKE4REPEAL, a grassroots feminist coalition that called for women to wear black and go on strike if the Irish government continued to delay a referendum were of working across borders and recognising a common ground from which to launch campaigns and demands.

What solidarity offers to feminist movements at the most basic level is more bodies to do the work. The work of raising awareness, of building consciousness, of petitioning, striking, blocking roads, bridges, towns, the work of shutting down hostile governments. More people engaged in struggle means the practical work of resistance might be achieved with new speed, new vigour or at the very least, a renewed energy. Solidarity refuses a narrow worldview and invites us to link our visions for the future to one another. It is also an affective experience: often it means bearing witness to the violence that takes place across the world and marking it where you are. In London 2019, members of the Sudanese Diaspora marked the violence and bloodshed of the ongoing revolution with vigils, including political readings, poetry and songs outside the European Commission. Solidarity can also be a site of healing, of naming your own complicity and refusing to remain silent.

There's no local without a global. There is no better answer to combat a fractured society obsessed with individualism than a politics that connects the dots. When we show solidarity to one another, we are demonstrating that we recognise that politics happens everywhere, at every level, in every region of the world. We break open the idea that feminism has a continental origin point; to recognise each other in struggle is to say, I *see* you, I understand that you have agency and because I cannot stand alongside you, I wish to bolster you from where I am. Solidarity, in an internationalist context, requires an emergent political practice. This means the ability to remain flexible in our responses and solutions; to listen to those on the ground and to redistribute resources.

When Carola Rackete, a German ship captain of the migrant NGO rescue ship Sea-Watch 3, rescued 43 migrants off the coast of Libya and defied Italian authorities to bring them into the Mediterranean Island of Lampedusa, she defied state orders and risked arrest to do so. Recognising that human life is more precious than the bureaucratic systems of power that are premised on its extinction is solidarity in action. Similarly, groups like Women on Waves, a Dutch non-profit organisation that sails boats to the coast of countries with the most restrictive abortion restrictions, picks up women and navigates them to international waters to provide free abortion pills and abortion support demonstrate that solidarity is an active, courageous principle. 'The fact that women need to leave the state sovereignty to retain their own sovereignty – it makes clear states are deliberately stopping women from accessing their human right to health,'[1] Leticia Zenevich told the Huffington Post. Anna Campbell, a 26-year-old woman from Bristol, was among seven British people who died volunteering for the YPJ, a group fighting ISIS based in Rojava in March 2018. She died after Turkish missiles struck her position, as she helped to evacuate citizens in Afrin. Solidarity requires us to *risk* something (our lives, citizenship, freedom) in order to support others; to put our theoretical principles to the test.

No bounds

Neha Shah, an anti-racist organiser tells me that her understanding of solidarity is informed by the knowledge that oppressive projects know no bounds and so, neither must our resistance:

---

1   www.huffingtonpost.in/entry/women-on-waves-abortion-boat_n_590b8338e4 b0d5d9049a857c (last accessed 07/2019).

Solidarity has to come from understanding, and understanding comes from listening to those who are in a position to know what they're talking about. The toxic effects of the colonial control of Palestinian land disproportionately harm women. Feminist solidarity in the Palestinian context has to start with listening to Palestinian women – for instance, with joining their call to organise against Donald Trump's so-called 'Deal of the Century' that seeks to disappear the Palestinian people and dismantle their collective rights, or heeding their call to campaign for boycotts, divestment and sanctions (BDS) against Israel.

For her, solidarity requires us to think beyond the nation:

There's a simple reason to think transnationally as feminists – if we don't, we give up one of our greatest strengths. The struggle for freedom is too difficult to embark on alone, and we share that struggle with women all over the world. Furthermore, feminism has to be transnational because patriarchy is transnational; we can't understand and resist the oppression of women as a group if we allow our analysis to stop at borders.

Solidarity can also help us think about the future. Elif Gun, active in the Kurdish women's movement, tells me that imagining a liberated future is closely linked to our ability to recognise each other in struggle:

A feminist future in my perspective is a struggle, because I honestly believe that without struggle and resistance life is not as beautiful, and I take this from Sakine Cansiz, one of the great minds behind the Kurdish women's movement. Without armed women, without women resisting always and continuously against the system, a feminist future is quite impossible, and a feminist future for me is only something we can achieve through active and collective resistance.

Looking outwards challenges the idea that politics revolves around the West and the people who live in it. While the power dynamics that underpin the organisation of the world often remain firmly in place because of the complicity of governments, something we must sit with and turn over in our heads, transnational solidarity offers us something. It offers us the ability to imagine that the world could be organised in a different way: it denaturalises the existence of borders, nations and states. To work in the spirit of common interest and mutual aid models the kind of world feminists are striving for: one that recognises that we would like to live as a collective rather than as individuals siphoned off into units. Call these units what you like: countries, continents, hemispheres or families. When we consider that nation states as we know them are relatively new inventions, we are reminded that our histories have always involved one another. Solidarity is a doing word – it offers us no blueprint or blindly optimistic visions for the future. It does not require us to always like each other or to erase the harm that might occur in our interpersonal interactions.

If solidarity can help us to find comfort in one another, it can also turn us into each other's worst nightmares. There are countless examples of the way that practices of solidarity have reduced the geopolitics of entire regions and continents for easy consumption. When Boko Haram kidnapped 276 girls from a secondary school in Chibok, Borno State, Nigeria in 2014, NGOs and public figures were quick to insert themselves into the narrative in an act of solidarity. 'Bring Back Our Girls' was the urgency of the political moment. Those on the outskirts of womanhood and the boundaries of flaccid, liberal politics have always been cast as the disrupters of political harmony. They introduce mess where an otherwise simple narrative might have been triumphant; they complicate that which should be easy. But feminism does not promise us easy answers. It promises us the hard work of seeing each other for all we are: including our faults, oversights and the ways we fail one another. In mainstream feminism, whiteness is central to that failure. When these oversights are addressed, solidarity is impeded by defensiveness and a refusal to recognise that women can be perpetrators of structural violence too. The terminology we use can also be a shield for other kinds of solidarities, obscuring for example, how 'women of colour' may enact anti-black coalitions that increase proximity to whiteness and reinforce hierarchies of being.

Womanhood, the central pillar under which we gather to make our demands, is not real. It is only a vantage point that we use strategically to lessen the brutality we experience. Lessening that brutality requires us not to be so preoccupied with harming one another that we forget who our enemies are. Once free, we might be free to hate each other, to deride solidarity, to argue that it does not work. But as long as we live under the conditions that we do, solidarity is one of the most important political tools we can use to maximise our success and make demands that cut across the structural barriers that seek to individualise our experiences. Individuals are right to be sceptical of the clumsy mobilisation of solidarity and attuned to its many failings. Perhaps a hopeful pessimism is our best chance – we organise across difference not because it solves our problems, but because the visions we seek to enact must be able to account for everyone. We are too involved in one another's lives, for better or worse. Chandra Mohanty argued 'the practice of solidarity foregrounds communities of people who have *chosen* to work and fight together.' She cites Jodi Dean, who argues that 'reflective solidarity' is crafted by an interaction involving three persons: 'I ask you to stand by me over me and against a third.'[2] Solidarity is a belief in one another that should be extended and rescinded accordingly. At the very least, it helps sharpen our focus on that *third*, who threatens our attempts to build a feminist future.

---

2   Chandra Mohanty, *Feminism Without Borders: Decolonizing Theory, Practicising Solidarity* (Durham: Duke University Press, 2003).

Conclusion

I hope I have made a compelling case for feminism as a social, political, economic and artistic framework for thinking collectively about our liberation. Feminism has the potential to transform the way we live, but first it must be untied from the neo-liberalism that blunts our imaginative faculties. In setting it free, we have to recognise that there are hard and complicated questions to answer about how to make the word liveable for *all* of us. This means paying close attention to the structures that organise our lives, committing ourselves to struggle and refusing the desire to simplify the task at hand. The violence of this world can seem at times overwhelming and all consuming, but it is important that we use feminism as one of the tools to make sense of it and to fight back through organising, movement building and grassroots rebellion. Whatever the outcome of our resistance is, whether or not we are alive to see our movements achieve their long and short-term goals, it is very important that we do it anyway. Resistance enables us to think about the future, it keeps us alive. I hope we all approach this task with the excitement and urgency it demands. Rejecting the illusion that liberal feminism offers us in favour of a radical politics is a life-long commitment.

Black feminists have always understood the importance of difference and tension. Those pushed to write from the margins and destitution; those who muddle and disrupt the traditional binary gender, those who have attempted to unsettle and dismantle 'them/us' binaries; writers and thinkers from the

CONCLUSION

Global South challenging Western hegemony and domination; those who are and have always been the wrong kind of woman . . . they have cleared a space for us to understand the political possibilities that feminism offers us. We only have to listen for it to reveal itself.

Resources

This is list is not prescriptive or exhaustive; it is only a starting point.

Organisations

SWARM (Sex Worker Advocacy Resistance Movement), a UK based collective of sex workers, part of a global movement demanding the decriminalisation of sex work.

The English Collective of Prostitutes, a network of sex workers working both on the streets and indoors campaigning for decriminalisation and safety.

Sisters Uncut, a feminist direct action group working against the closure of domestic violence services and other forms of state violence.

Feminist Fightback, an anti-capitalist feminist collective.

Women's Strike Assembly, a radical collective co-coordinating the annual women's strike.

Wretched of The Earth, a collective of over a dozen grassroots Indigenous, black, brown and diaspora groups, individuals and allies acting in solidarity with oppressed communities in the Global South and Indigenous North.

Black Lives Matter UK, a grassroots coalition organising against systematic racism and state violence against black people.

INQUEST, the only charity in the UK providing expertise on state-related deaths and their investigation to bereaved people, lawyers, advice and support agencies, the media and parliamentarians.

Feminist Antifacist Assembly, a radical collective of feminists fighting against the racist and sexist ideas of the far right.

My Body Back, an organisation that supports women who have experienced rape or sexual assault to love and care for their bodies again.

CAPE (Community Action Against Prisons), a network of grassroots groups fighting prison expansion in England, Wales and Scotland.

RESOURCES

Abortion Support Network provides advice on travelling for abortion, financial assistance towards the costs, and, where needed and where possible, accommodation in volunteer homes.

Mermaids, a national charity working to support young transgender and gender diverse people, their parents and their communities.

Books

Stella Dadzie, Susanne Scafe and Beverley Bryan, *The Heart of the Race: Black Women's Lives in Britain* (Verso, 2018).

Angela Davis, *Women Race and Class* (Ballatine Books, 1983).

Angela Davis, *Are Prisons Obsolete?* (Seven Stories Press, 2003).

Nancy Fraser, Cinzia Arruzza and Tithi Bhattacharya, *Feminism for the 99%* (Verso, 2019).

Sakine Cansiz, *Sara: A Prison Memoir of a Kurdish Revolutionary*, translated and edited by Janet Biehl (Pluto Press, 2019).

bell hooks, *Feminism is for Everybody: Passionate Politics* (Pluto Press, 2000).

Dawn Foster, *Lean Out* (Repeater Books, 2016).

Juno Mac and Molly Smith, *Revolting Prostitutes: The Fight for Sex Workers' Rights* (Verso, 2018).

Audre Lorde, *Sister Outsider* (Penguin, 2019).

Julia Sudbury, *Other Kinds of Dreams: Black Women's Organisations and the Politics of Transformation* (Gender, Racism, Ethnicity) (Routledge, 1998).

Carol Boyce Davies, *Left of Karl Marx: The Political Life of Black Communist Claudia Jones* (Duke University Press, 2008).

Sara Ahmed, *Living a Feminist Life* (Duke University Press, 2017).

Barbara Smith (ed), 'Combahee River Collective Statement', in *Home Girls, A Black Feminist Anthology* (Kitchen Table: Women of Color Press, 1983).

Julia Serano, *Whipping Girl: A Transsexual Woman on Sexism and the Scapegoating of Femininity* (Seal Press, 2007).

Silvia Federeci, *Caliban and The Witch: Women, the Body and Primitive Accumulation* (Autonomedia, 2017).

Hartman, S. (2019) *Wayward Lives, Beautiful Experiments*. New York: WW Norton & Company.

Nash, J.C. (2019) *Black Feminism Reimagined: After Intersectionality*. Durham: Duke University Press.

Emejulu, Akwugo and Francesca Sobande, editors. *To Exist Is to Resist: Black Feminism in Europe*. Pluto Press, 2019.

Archives

British Library 'Sisterhood and After' Collection
Black Cultural Archives
The Feminist Review Archive
The Feminist Library
East End Women's Museum

Poets/artists/zine-makers

Faith Ringgold
Black Women's Group – Brixton Art Collective
Carrie Mae Weems
Victoria Sin
Hannah Black
Mona Hatoum
Barby Asante
Jay Bernard
The White Pube
OOMK (One of My Kind)
The Khidr Collective
Daikon
Momtaza Mehri
Zanele Muholi
Travis Alabanza
Sonia Boyce

The Pluto Press Newsletter

Hello friend of Pluto!

Want to stay on top of the best radical books
we publish?

Then sign up to be the first to hear about our
new books, as well as special events,
podcasts and videos.

You'll also get 50% off your first order with us
when you sign up.

Come and join us!

Go to bit.ly/PlutoNewsletter